A Hasti... ...te
The Reprob... ...gy • 1

Derek Loveland

A HASTINGS REPROBATE
THE REPROBATE TRILOGY • 1

Copyright © 2020 Derek Loveland
First Published in Great Britain in 2020 by
Reprobate Books,
71 Queen's Road, Hastings
East Sussex, TN34 1RL, UK
Email: reprobatebooks@gmail.com

Fiction (based on a true story)
ISBN 978-1-873976-98-2
British Cataloguing in Publication Data
A catalogue record for this book is available from the British Library

All rights reserved. No part of this publication may be reproduced or transmitted in any form or by any means, electronic or mechanical, including photocopy, recording or any information storage and retrieval system now know or to be invented, without permission in writing from the publisher, except by a reviewer who wishes to quote brief passages in connection with a review written for inclusion in a magazine, newspaper, or broadcast.

Names and Characters are the product of the author's imagination and any resemblance to actual persons, living or dead, is entirely co-incidental.

Printed on Paper from sustainable managed forests
by Printed Word Publishing
Burgess Road, Hastings, East Sussex TN35 4NR

Part of the
scantech
EFFECTIVE COMMUNICATION GROUP

anti-slavery Lifeboats

Acknowledgements

To Linda, who put up with my back turned while I sat in a corner writing the book.

To Sheila J. Martin for her patience in trying to make sense of the manuscript, then turning it into something readable.

To Richard Buckley for his help with the grammar and advice with the cover illustration.

To Stuart Christie, without whose encouragement, after a chance encounter in the Junk Shop, my life-story would have remained untold. Stuart is the author of '*Granny Made Me an Anarchist*' and many other absorbing works.

Other Books Available

The Reprobate • Trilogy • 2
The Reprobate in Sweden

The Reprobate • Trilogy • 3
The Reprobate in the Antiques Trade

Drawing by R. A. Buckley

ADVERTISEMENT

PWP

PRINTED WORD PUBLISHING

Printed Word Publishing is your Hastings book printing company. If you need any help in designing and / or publishing your book they are the company to go to.

**Contact Eddie Sturgeon
on 01424 722733 or
email: eddie@scan-tech.co.uk**

SO FAR SO GOOD

At Hastings Rail station in the middle of October 1965 with my mother by my side, on platform three, standing behind the white line that separates safety from harm, I closed my left eye so I could concentrate fully, reciting over and over again in my mind the lyrics 'I'm Free 'by 'The Who.' The Sixties cultural revolution was the perfect period for me to form an identity, giving me confidence to voice an opinion, create new ideas and express aloud feelings of personal issues and heartfelt desires. I call myself Zac At just fifteen and a half I was leaving home for the first time, having left 'Hastings Secondary School for Boys' with no formal qualifications or any sense of purpose, plus a hearing defect in my left ear as a result of a punishment-injury acquired during my infant years.

The previous evening as I lay on my bed staring at the ceiling, I realized this was to be my last night in my bedroom. I knew that I had in me the 'wanderlust gene', a trait most probably inherited from my estranged birth-mother. For years I have been aware of my inability to concentrate or to prevent my mind wandering off in obscure directions. That night I tried to calm my foster father and make it clear to him that his family were not to blame, it was entirely my fault that I wanted to leave home, not theirs. He nodded his head in agreement and then announced he had to go to work, he was a sales rep in Eastbourne, starting at an unreasonably early hour in the morning. True to his word by the time I came down for breakfast he was gone; perfect timing. My 'brother', David two years my senior, came to see me off, just before going to work as a Housing officer for Hastings Borough County Council. David their natural son with whom I got on well wished me luck.

My 'mother' and I were in the kitchen, not really acknowledging each other's presence whilst we took breakfast together. She gave me an extra-large portion, bringing to my mind 'Jesus at the Last Supper'. I watched her as she cleared the table. I offered to dry the dishes, always a foregone conclusion a task I enjoyed, my mother was also upset by my impending departure, still I went about my business with a tea towel in hand. A few years earlier we would have listened and sung along to the voice of her second love, Mario Lanza, the greatest tenor of the time.

I saw in my mind's eye, (with my left eye shut), a final opportunity to look at her, just over five foot and of slim build, always complaining about her large backside. She was an awful dancer, with no sense of rhythm, yet of smart formal appearance, with her regular hairdresser's idea of the latest fashion: an old-style 'perm', held firmly in place.

We left the house; she slammed the front door and turned the key, then with a familiar sideways glare informed me that under no circumstances should I dare to try to engage in any form of conversation with her.

Behind me I took in a familiar view towards the Old Town, fishing boats on the stony beach at Rock-a-Nore, where the local fishermen were taking a well-earned rest from the previous night's fishing on the harsh high tides in the English Channel. I recalled my best school friend Frank, who came from a council house in Hardwick Road; this was frowned upon by my mother; however Frank and I would often go on Saturday afternoons to visit his grandparent's small terraced cottage in Tackleway, where outside toilets were nestled together in a straight line in the open courtyard.

The front door was always open and upon seeing her grandson, without hesitation the fisherman's wife would invite us in and indulge us in mugs of tea, fresh sandwiches and homemade cakes. Although it was apparent that funds were low, owing to foreign frozen fish imports and the rising cost of living, she would always show us hospitality and say that, as growing boys we should eat till our heart's content.

When her husband was at home, having been restrained from his days work owing to treacherous weather conditions at sea, he would tell us nefarious seafaring stories, true or not, nevertheless we were in awe of the old mans' tales of woe and fortitude. The following year, this being our fourteenth year of age or thereabouts and owing to our sudden interest in girls, we eventually saw less of Frank's grandparents.

As Frank was related to the fishing community, strong for his age, he would on occasion assist the landing of the fishing boats; he declined the offer of the 'boy ashore' role owing to the nature of having to work such long hours in hazardous conditions for a very low income.

Leaving school just after his fifteenth birthday, Frank was taken on as an apprentice plumber with British Gas, riding an old bike carrying the work bag of tools from one job to another. Able to complete his five year apprentice on low wages, Frank gained the status of a fully qualified gas central heating engineer, eventually appointed as a foreman and area-training-manager, staying with the same company for many years.

TUBMAN BIDDY

One afternoon sitting on the pebble beach I took in the sight of the infamous Tubman Biddy, with paddle in hand, beating away the tides waves trying to row the empty oak wooden beer barrel, his idea of a seaworthy vessel. With all his strength he attempted to climb into it to stay afloat and paddle a short distance. A renowned showman with the courage of his conviction, always seen wearing a broad smile from ear to ear, in the hope of receiving small change as his just reward from an audience of holiday-makers who sat on the pebble beach, clapping and cheering at such a spectacle with adoration, coming from far and wide, just to see one of the Old Town's favourite seaside entertainers.

I caught sight of the entertainer on his way home, taking a rest sitting on our front garden wall soaked to the skin, the oak barrel by his side he was checking his trouser pockets for cash, his smile to himself spoke volumes, a good afternoon was had by all. My family's home in Collier Road passed into Bembrook Road where at that period in time; a high wall existed dividing the two roads. Eventually the council removed the wall much to the annoyance of my mother, as council house tenants she remarked would lower the value of Collier road.

Looking towards the East Hill silhouetted on the cliffs edge is one of the last public lifts still in operation in the country. On the cliff face a ravine cut by the labour force of a bygone age, setting steel rails at a steep angle for the wooden carriages to go up and down in unison on-board carrying an ever increasing amount of holiday makers. Now at the summer seasons end put out of commission for the winter period, for maintenance work to be carried out.

I remember in my adolescence, about two years ago with Frank and a gang of friends on Saturday afternoons, we would be found loitering in an Amusement Arcade along George Street and then pass through the wide open side street towards the seafront along to the popular Promenade fish and chip restaurant opposite the entrance to the West hill Lift, annoying the mother of two teen-aged daughters where they worked at weekends for pocket money, trying to encourage them to pass through the hatch window a large portion of chips for free that we would all share in.

Afterwards climbing the hundred steps up to the West Hill cliffs, with penknives in hand we carved into the sand rock cliff face our interpretation of a heart, announcing our undying love for the girl of our dreams. Next we would play 'kiss and tell', trying to induce the girls into a cave, our 'den of iniquity', lighting a small bonfire and often smoking cigarettes. If the girls entered into the cave we tried to have our wicked way, closed-mouth kissing this was our way of petting.

I frequently walked down the path into 'Wallinger's Walk', past the Victorian decaying graveyard, sighting to my left Hastings Castle a relic of the past, a feature that encourages visitors from all around the world to take in the whole atmosphere of the 1066 period. Across the road was the open aperture of the well-maintained 'Wellington Gardens', down into Queen's Road in sight of the 'Pam-Dor' coffee bar. A place, for the youth of the day, I frequented that place many times with friends, listening to the latest hits on an old 'Rock-Ola' Juke Box, the overused steel needle forever scratching the vinyl's surface.

Often I played pinball, causing it to nudge thus bringing

the game to a premature end. As my testosterone level was running high causing me anxiety I found the plug in the wall socket and rendered it out of action. At the spring of life, I ventured into the art of frivolity with my schoolmates looking at the girls wearing the latest fashion, 'Mary Quant' hairstyles, fish net stockings, revealing flesh just below the suspender belt in the shortest of skirts imaginable.

On arrival at the railway station, after our unhurried twenty-five minute walk, we went to the ticket office and stood behind a short orderly queue.

'One single child's ticket to London Victoria and one adult 'cheap day return' please,' my mother asked in her usual polite manner to the lone counter staff. Raising himself to his full height, peering down at us in an authoritarian manner, he inquired of my age, telling her that if I was over sixteen the full fare must be paid. My 'mother' replied in a polite manner, stating that I had just left school and adding that I was aged fifteen and a quarter, proof of this could be offered to him if necessary.

The ticket clerk informed us in an obnoxious way, that it was his duty to tell us that we were not allowed to travel before a specific time, as the cheap day tickets were only valid after nine fifteen; these were British Rail's rules, he was to make the general public aware of this fact, if found boarding before the allotted time and caught a fine would be set in motion. I listened to him in his nonchalant manner towards my mother and thought that he should do us all a great service and take early retirement!

One thing is for sure; my foster parents gave me virtually every useful set of tools to survive life, exemplary table manners, clean personal habits and elocution lessons paid for by The Social Services.

Catching the permitted train and speaking to my mother 'That's good the train is right on time', offering my hand to help her to board, whilst avoiding the treacherous gap between the platform and the open door to an empty compartment was to no avail, she just responded coldly towards me.

I was hurt by her attitude, as a few years ago up until the age of about thirteen; I and only I would walk by her side to the church in the woods graveyard in the Hollington area of St Leonard's-on-sea. Every Sunday afternoon we would walk the quarter of a mile to visit her mother's grave. My 'grandmother' died at only sixty one, I think the probable cause was cancer of the larynx, my diagnosis was her chain-smoking cigarettes, also assisted by the spores lurking beneath the old damp wallpaper, conditions that took hold in our old four-storey tenanted house on Bohemia Road. This was a short walk to my Primary School in St. Paul s Road close by St Peters Church, where I was a choirboy attending both morning and evening services every Sunday for many years. No family members at home ever attended church, not even at Christmas or any other period of religious festivity.

My religious duties were down to my birth mother's wishes, where she would wield her power through the help of the Social Services in Strathclyde, from her home in Govan, Glasgow Scotland.

She enforced one stipulation, that I was not allowed to be adopted, even if anyone wanted to take me on as their unpaid responsibility, also she had the notion to change her mind in relation to my religious upbringing. One day a Catholic, then a Jew like her and at some point a Quaker. Ultimately for at least eight years a regular member at St. Peters Church just off

Bohemia road on the corner of Chapel Park Road.

No adoption and those various religious experiences were the only two factors that were under her control; she never came to see me, no phone calls, Christmas or birthday cards, or anything else that could be normal for a child. To my surprise before the end of my schooldays just before my fifteenth birthday, a letter from her was forwarded on to me, after having been vetted by my Social worker. I became excited at the thought of her sudden interest in my very existence and to see a letter written in her own handwriting offering me the chance to look for some sort of similarity between us, as the written word in long-hand can speak volumes.

However this was not to be, as the man she was living with at the time had written it on her behalf, the excuse being that she was not up to it on that particular day. I was informed that as soon as I was of employment age she requested that I should move to Glasgow and live with her, as help towards the housekeeping would be most welcome.

The only thing I gained from my biological mother was the need to travel, knowing that if I am unhappy in any given situation I urge to go forward into the unknown, towards the light and dark of life.

Though reluctant, I am following her in a similar way, though miles apart and never-ever having had any physical communication. Nevertheless we have both been in institutions, I in children's homes and she as a regular voluntary patient in a Psychiatric Institution in Glasgow, able to be free to come and go as her needs required.

One day she turned up without an appointment or a Doctors referral. However after a few days a member of staff, who had known her from the past, inquired as to the whereabouts of her young children, 'No problem,' she responded, 'The children are at home, taking care of each other, anyway my eleven year old son is in charge and looking after them.'

THE TRAIN JOURNEY

The train left at the exact time scheduled, as it started from Hastings all carriages and most seats were empty. We settled into an eight-seater compartment, I chose to sit at the window; she took the seat opposite to me. Window positions are the best if you wish to avoid making eye contact. Our first stop through a long tunnel was Warrior Square station, a few passengers boarded, there were only vacant seats in our carriage and still no conversation was held between us.

After a while I gazed out of the window, the drizzle of the rain taking some immediate view from me, nevertheless in no time at all I relaxed as the trains rocking motion from side to side steadied my nerves, allowing me to take comfort in the situation that I found myself in. Out of ear-shot of any passengers I tried in vain to break the silence, but her hands were clenched together so tightly on her lap that the blood supply to the end of her fingertips showed pink. Blue veins were raised in lines across the top of her hands; her right leg below the knee was shaking out of control.

Next stop Bexhill; we were still in an empty compartment, other passengers would be most welcome to break the impasse. Arriving at Eastbourne station only one scruffy old man entered our compartment, he rescued from the litter bin a broadsheet newspaper, holding it wide open in front of his face to avoid eye contact; he remained in a state of anonymity until he departed at Tunbridge Wells' station, bidding a farewell to us before we were able to acknowledge him in the same manner.

I was taken by surprise owing to the trains' diversion, a delight before my eyes to see passengers' en-mass coming in our direction starting to board the train. Leather briefcases in hand, the obligatory pin-striped suits and custom-made bowler-hatted city gents, women in their formal work attire, skirts rising daily due to the latest fashion, showing off their long legs in stiletto black high heel shoes, wearing flesh coloured nylon stockings, the seductive straight black line to the back, demanding men to salivate over the fleeting moment.

Everyone was talking to each other, taking the opportunity for once to converse with a fellow passenger and to moan at the poor service British Rail offered. At long last we were not alone, standing room only. A heavily pregnant mother with a small child by her side, jostled around in an uncomfortable way owing to the diesel trains high speed, without any hesitation I offered my seat to her she was grateful for this; which allowed me to squeeze past passengers into the corridor to be alone, to gather my thoughts.

The train came to a halt by the wooden rectangle placard in black and white lettering, 'Clapham Junction'. An announcer in a fractured voice was transmitting information from the Tannoy system, 'Next stop London Victoria.' I was just able to understand his announcement; it was a deep male voice from overseas and owing to my hearing defect in my left ear caused me irritation.

My notes state, so I am informed, that this was inflicted on me between the age of two and four years, a slap to the side of my head caused the minor disability, a form of natural punishment on a regular basis, quite normal for the period early nineteen fifties. I suspect I was a nuisance, a relentless fidget and an incessant chatterbox, added to which my speech impediment was out of control, this must have caused aggravation to some of the members of staff at the Children's Home.

We arrived at Victoria station with a sudden jolt, the train hit the buffers at an alarming speed causing us to collide with one another; however the regular commuters just sighed, remarking, 'It's a regular occurrence.' After the impact, the train stopped safely and I took the opportunity to make conversation. 'That's good were right on time,' I waited for an answer, no reply came. I reached above my head into the luggage rack to collect my belongings, a blue hold-all bag with my entire possessions held within. I took the lead to open the steel slam door; other passengers passed me to alight on to the safety of the platform. 'Let's follow them mum', I paused to take charge of my emotion, 'Can you get the tickets mum, maybe best to get them ready if you don't mind,' of course I had asked her this only a few minutes ago, now I was repeating myself and not in an audible way. I was hoping for some sort of reaction, she just looked at me with distaste, replying 'This is horrible,' in a hoarse whisper.

We were the last to get off bar one other passenger, a smart city gentlemen middle aged, stocky in stature, pale face of no redeeming features with a fine perfectly-fitted bowler hat, motioned us to take a position in front of him, an act of chivalry and manners of the day. My mother reacted with pursed lips, a terse message of thanks; he in return touched the brim of his hat in response. We were sandwiched moving towards the front of the train, ready to plant ourselves outside onto the stations' platform. Both moving slowly in a huddled way towards the ticket barrier gate; I was just behind her, as there was no other option.

At the ticket barriers, two male inspectors stood eight feet apart, with no interest in their work whatsoever, not even looking at the validity of tickets or anything else for that matter. A good thing for us I surmised, as she hadn't even got the tickets out ready for inspection.

In the middle of Victoria Railway Station next to the Tourist Information office, I felt nervous and disoriented about the consequences of my former decision, in coming to such a place and to find myself in such a crowded environment, the noise was so deafening, causing me to feel overpowered and very nauseous.

Uniformed military soldiers on leave, city gents carrying leather briefcases, their shoes polished to a mirror finish and mothers pushing their new 'Silver Cross' perambulators, weaving their way in earnest, trying to avoid those in their way. Immigrants from all corners of the globe, suitcases in hand in search of a better way of life in England.

PARTING OF THE WAYS

A little earlier Dr Dylen had arrived in Hastings for an emergency meeting in order to understand my reasons for wanting to move to London.

For the previous four months immediately after leaving school, I found a job working at a restaurant opposite Hastings Pier as a kitchen porter working in the basement, washing huge greasy pots and pans and a never-ending supply of dirty dishes, all by hand. Six days a week, twelve hours a day, with a one hours break if it was a quiet period.

One afternoon on my break I noticed a casual market trader at the pier entrance; he was selling luggage, belts, tobacco pouches, wallets and a variety of other leather goods. My eyes were drawn to a large navy blue hold-all bag with leather handles, which looked somewhat 'the worse for wear'. The salesman winked and said it had fallen off the back of a lorry but that it was tough and strong enough to travel the world over. He had drawn me into his story and offered it at a reduced price, I then purchased it.

Standing together my mother and I made eye contact, then she screamed so loud her cry was deafening, 'Look at me Zechariah, this is horrible; stop this at once and listen to me, don't you dare move away from me, I'm so sorry but I can't help it, I think I'm so much of a failure, your father said the same thing this morning that he and David will miss you so much'. Now muttering, unaware that a large crowd has formed, they were staring at us in amazement, 'It's still not too late to turn back,' pleading with me in a low tone of voice, I interrupted her raising my voice to a high pitch.

'Things will be okay, anyway it's not your fault it's mine, I don't know how to explain myself.'

We were fast becoming a spectacle of curiosity in-front of voyeurs, the general public passing time by gossiping about us before going about their daily routine. She was in a poor way, unaware were in the middle of an ever-increasing rowdy crowd causing me to feel claustrophobic. Taking the initiative, attempting to reassure her I put my hand on her shoulder, but my actions seem to make things worse as now her screaming became intolerable, she tried to pull me towards her, gripping my wrist in an aggressive manner causing me pain.

With tears smearing her blue eye-shadow, bright cherry-red gloss lipstick staining the top set of her teeth and trembling lips out-of-control she screamed,

'What's all this rubbish about, your wanting to shorten your name to Zac? Zechariah is your name who on earth gave you that idea? I suppose one of your stupid friends; you really are so young and foolish.'

I shouted at her, 'For your information, in my eyes you are my mum and anyway Zechariah is so old-fashioned these days, I want to forget that awful birth-mother woman in Scotland who gave me that stupid name, she had no right to give me any name, sorry mum it's not you, it's all my fault'.

She stared at me in a state of bewilderment. 'Now listen to me young man, if you really must call yourself 'Zac' or whatever, maybe I could get used to it but you really have let our good name down, what will the neighbours think they will laugh at us', pausing for breath, 'Leaving us just after you have finished school I thought you cared about us and would get a job and follow in David's footsteps' I interrupted in a tone of defiance, 'I don't care about the neighbours and what they think, anyway look over there its Dr. Dylen and he's spotted us.'

In the distance above the eye-line of the growing crowd, he stood on tiptoe to add inches to his height of just over six-foot tall, fair hair pushed to one side, thick lips, broken nose, which he informed me at our one and only prior meeting, was down to his love of playing rugby. Dr. Dylen had blue eyes and pale-to-sallow complexion; he wore a pinstripe double-breasted suit and sported a familiar Cambridge University tie.

A determination about him, taking long strides to form a path in an aggressive manner, making the crowd take notice and divide, the circle around us was broken. Not only were we fixed in position making it difficult for us to move in any direction whatsoever, murmurs of nasty boy, give him a good hiding, poor woman, so on so forth were now being shouted at us, the watchers had stopped standing in silence, it felt like a mob situation.

The crowd let him pass, as they saw his open hand held out to greet us. The Director of Social Services in the Borough of Lambeth chose to get involved with my case as it was unusual for a boy of such a young age to want to return to a Children's Home in London, having lived with the same foster parents in Hastings for around ten years asking to move back London, without any family connection.

'Good to see you both', he greeted us in his clipped Public School accented voice.

'Talk to him Dr. Dylen, make him come home, you know it makes sense, anyway he's got it in his mind that he now wants to be called, Zac'. Her next sentence was incoherent and impossible for him to understand.

Dr Dylen could see her shaking and in a state of utter despair, her nervous system failing her. I had witnessed this a few times before, at least for the last past six years. Since her mother passed away, she had been prescribed Valium and Librium, by her G.P. she was at the end of her tether, trembling fingers, screaming and crying all amplified the chaos in her mind.

'I will ring every week, I promise, on Sunday evening around seven o'clock; anyway it's for the best.' I rested my hand on her shoulder again, her body language rigid, ordering me to keep my distance.

'You never ever cared about me, it's your entire fault, I should have taken another child, certainly not you.'

With this she turned around to face three uniformed British Rail police officers, one young female officer accompanied by two male colleagues, both middle aged, they were attempting to disperse the crowd who were muttering and making derogatory remarks about us, our distress witnessed before their very eyes at one point staring at me in a menacing way. Then a couple of elderly women started to voice their opinions, advising my mother that she should give me a good hiding, that the youth of today should be taken in hand, do as their told and respect their elders.

The young officer spoke first; she had a mild manner, her two senior colleagues just observed as she offered assistance to my mother. She asked for a show of tickets. My mother responded to her request and fumbled in her handbag as its contents spilled to the floor. Finding her valid tickets the officer without hesitation informed us that everything was in order.

The rail officials quizzed Dr. Dylen, asking for proof of his identity, enquiring why he was there. Acknowledging their request he produced his credentials of high office, with many letters after his name, impressed with the high position he held the officials were placated.

After a request to her male colleagues, regarding the fact that she was in such a terrible state, oblivious to her immediate surrounding's, the female officer volunteered to ensure my mother's safe return to Hastings. The suggestion was agreed unanimously and they commended the lady's suggestion.

My mother had removed her shoes and in her stocking feet, started running away from me. I shouted at her, 'Don't forget Sunday evening, I will call you mum,' in my broken adolescent voice, she hesitated and I knew from her moment of hesitation, that she had heard me; I knew I had to let go of her and she of me.

The two remaining officers advised Dr Dylen that after such a disturbance, with the public complaining and alarmed at the spectacle where B.R. staff took a long time to intervene, they had to make a full written report of the incident. They would require him to co-operate with the British rail transport police as the matter had been reported to them also and was being taken seriously.

The officers additionally took me to one side to verify that I in fact knew Dr Dylen, and to take my name and address in Hastings's for future reference. Satisfied with my answers I was allowed to re-join Dr Dylen; he suggested that we should go to a self-service café at the station and take some refreshment saying that I must be in need of food after the recent ordeal, adding that the Social Services department would pay for everything.

I voiced concerns about my mother boarding the train for the return journey home, with brand new shoes in one hand, attempting to get on the train without my help, what if she were to lose her sense of balance and fall into the wide gap below and injure or kill herself.

Dr Dylen assured me that mother was in safe hands and would be accompanied back safely and that this was of paramount importance to the British Rail staff.

Sitting by the window in the same compartment as before, grief-stricken, ashamed of her behaviour and trying to come to terms with the outcome of the day's events, my mother soon realised that she was now minus one son, a foster child that, until his thirteenth birthday, she had loved and been kind to, but of late had become difficult and hard to control.

Seeing her grief-stricken reflection in the window gave mother a sharp shock, awakening her senses, she took out of her handbag a compact and powdered her face in such a rage that a thick tidemark around her neck bore witness to the event. Her lips retouched with lipstick was applied in a state of extreme anguish, which recalled to my mind the face of the woman in the painting by Picasso, the 'Weeping Woman' an abstract 'Cubist' form of modern Art.

The young officer sitting next to her, first observed and then held her hand for the whole of the journey, total silence was in place; at the journeys end my mother spoke for the first time, thanking the officer for her gratitude and kindness towards her.

Arriving on time she was stopped by an inspector asking to check her tickets. Fumbling in her brand new handbag, without any form of co-ordination, the contents spilled to the ground, then looking up she was taken aback by the appearance of the same clerk who had served her on the morning journey.

The female officer based at Victoria identified herself to the Hastings station staff and watched as her charge left the station; her duty done.

A member of staff hailed a black cab for mother and she was gone.

Seated on the back seat she was talking to herself again, repeating again and again to the driver, 'You know my dear, I'm going to foster a small child and the little darling will be all mine.'

Back home again my foster mother sat in her 1950's armchair, a blanket over her knees, feet resting on a late-Victorian wooden stool upholstered on top with 'petit point' needlework. An early period mahogany wine table with a carved cabriolet base was by her side. A glass of water on a table mat stood on the wine table with two glass bottles of tablets, one marked 'L' the other 'V' either or both took over her thoughts of her presence in the world, she gazed at the familiar view toward the East Hill, with its brown, autumnal bracken carpet, visible in the distance.

FIRST COUSIN ONCE REMOVED

Stacking my tray high with food, encouraged by Dr. Dylen, I do like my food, I recall how at school dinners I was always the first in line asking for 'More seconds please!' Regardless of how much I eat, I never seemed to put on weight. I am one of life's fidgets, I have an inkling that my high nervous energy may keep my weight down but often causes irritation to those in my company. Dr. Dylen also had a good appetite, so with this in mind I feel not an ounce of guilt in helping myself to even more food, anyway London county council are footing the bill through his expense account.

On the floor around our table the amount of cigarette end's and pieces of half-eaten food, made me think about the horrible domestic habits of the previous diners.

A young black teenager, scruffy in appearance, not in work uniform that should have been provided by his employers, was slouching around with his broom in one hand and a dirty dish cloth in the other, all the time his eyes were fixed towards the circular analogue clock. Having noticed that we were occupying a dirty vacant table he approached us; we moved the red plastic stacking chairs to one side as he swept under the table. I thanked him and in response he turned towards me, his eyes open wide, complemented by a shy smile. After having eaten in silence Dr Dylen and I smiled at each other, so meeting of minds perhaps. Dr. Dylen then broke the silence.

'Zac or shall I refer to you as Zechariah?' Looking at him 'If you don't mind I do prefer Zac as this is the start of a new life.' After an uncomfortable pause Dr. Dylen said 'You must never under any circumstance use the name Zac in any legal situation, it could amount to be a criminal offence. Do you understand?'

I replied 'Thanks, I understand what you mean; by the way you're the first person to call me Zac outside my friends, mum hates it, thanks for that.'

'Let's move on and have a chat about where you will be living from now on. As you know it's in South-East London at a National Children's Home for seven to sixteen years old, or in exceptional circumstance two years older. Remember Zac, your sixteenth birthday is in nine months' time, then you must leave and find somewhere else to live, outside the care of the local authorities, you will have to fend for yourself."

I held my hand to my left ear in order to hear his every word, Dr. Dylen, acknowledging my slight hearing problem said 'We can go elsewhere if it is too noisy in here'. We decided to stay at the cafe as it was settling down into the quieter part of the afternoon.

I changed the subject:

'How was your holiday in South America? Sorry I don't mean to be nosy but didn't you tell me that was where you and your wife were going?'

He replied. 'Yes, we did go to Brazil, but this meeting is about you, your aspirations and so on, what are your future plans, have you made any?'

'No not really,'

'Have you thought about going into further education? If you're interested I may be able to steer you in the right direction. All you have to do is to decide what kind of training for a job you might want, they may even allow you to live at the home until you're eighteen, if you are in education they make certain allowances, I want you to consider your options. I notice that at secondary school aged between eleven to fifteen, you came second to bottom of the class out of thirty-two other boys, but what I don't understand is that when you were thirteen you came second to the top of the class in English literature and third in math's. So my question is why didn't you just carry on? And while on this subject it was in your school report that every teacher observed that you have a lot of potential, but for some unknown reason you seemed to be caught looking out of the window, as if staring into space.'

I didn't want to respond to this line of questioning, so I shrugged my shoulders and tightened my lips.

'My mouth's dry and I can see you nodding off soon, come on Zac wake up; let's have another cup of tea.'

We both chuckle out loud putting me at ease again, not for a while had I felt so relaxed and jolly especially in the company of any other Social Worker; he was definitely the best one I ever had, as he talked to me not down to me.

As the atmosphere was gentle between us I asked Dr Dylen 'If you don't mind me asking, have you any children? Sorry if I've spoken out of turn, I don't mean to pry'.

'It's not a problem for me, it's only natural that you should ask questions, I have nothing to hide.' he smiled with a quirky sort of grin, 'No children, so far, not for the want of trying though.'

I notice he started to blush through his pale complexion, I looked away to save him from embarrassment

'Where was I? Sarah, my wife is an anesthetist at the Royal Free Hospital in Hampstead, North London. We moved from Wandsworth to be close to her work, she works such awfully long hours doing shift work, bad for one's health you know!'

Then I asked, 'Did you have a nice holiday?'

'Indeed, it took our minds off work. But think on what I said just now, on the importance of formal qualifications. As for my holiday in August, we had spent our time looking after the children in an orphanage; one might say a bus-man's holiday, am I boring you?'

'No, not at all, I'm really interested!'

He replied, with his left eye-brow raised. 'So where was I?' He held the palms of both hands open for effect.

'For the last eight years, Sarah and I have arranged our work-schedules so that we can take holidays together. For three weeks around August-September time, we go abroad when the temperature is not too high, having a fair complexion I sunburn easily.

After an exhausting but rewarding night spent in search of stray children, we returned to a shared house where we all contributed towards the shopping, taking turns at cooking which was a delight and quite informative, where different cuisine through other cultures can be sampled, amusing stories exchanged, an interesting way of life —spiritually uplifting.

You see Zac, toward the twilight hours we go off looking for young children, the so called gutter children, in Rio de Janeiro. The wretched tiny children, some as young as four or even younger I guess, have been discarded by their mothers, most are illiterate and often the mothers have suffered rape and endured living in squalid conditions, by a hand to mouth existence. So the destitute children are almost everywhere except in the wealthiest suburbs of that ever-expanding city.

Some dreadful people with evil and warped minds shoot them like common vermin, not dissimilar to sewer rats, to stop them disturbing the valuable tourist trade, safe clean streets and the American way of living brings much-needed currency into the capital.

We try to offer the children a safe haven at a well-run orphanage, where they are out of reach of such predators and with patience and encouragement teach them to read and write, learning good habits and able to integrate into society, also to respect each other.'

Sipping tea, after taking three teaspoonful of sugar, then stirring and tapping the cups edge three times, is a habit of his I observe.

'I work for a charitable organisation set up through donations from the wealthiest philanthropists to assist the poorest members of society.'

I stopped him 'What does that long word mean, sorry for interrupting you?' He reacted earnestly.

'Rich people give money to the needy of our society. Another form of giving is where a person has chosen to live and work for no financial gain helping others.

Calcutta, India, is where Mother Theresa an Albanian nun, I think, dedicated her life freely, helping on a daily basis, the poorest and sickest children, giving them comfort and hope — in my view the humblest of persons imaginable. Mother Theresa has given one hundred percent of her life in the quest of helping the less fortunate; compared to her Sarah and I are just part-timers. At the end of our three weeks' vacation we return home to our comfortable lives. One's duty is to be charitable to others, in giving charity it's returned with a smile that enters deep into our heart, so let that be a lesson to you young man. I'm waiting in earnest to listen to your next question as I'm aware you have such an inquiring mind?' He smiled a glorious smile to stretch to eternity.

'Yes, you're right Dr Dylen can I ask you a personal

question?'

He was on his guard; after all he is my superior, for the first time an uncomfortable feeling was in the air.

'Go ahead, put your question to me, of course I will not submit an answer if I feel it to be inappropriate, you do understand that don't you?'

Tentatively I put my next question, before asking him I closed my left eye tight, to allow me to concentrate my train of thought.

'Are you a member of CND — ban the bomb and all that stuff? A few friends of mine in Hastings have got the round sign stitched on Levis or Wrangler jeans and drawn on school bags.'

His mouth opened, showing off his perfect white teeth. 'Now you really have touched on one of my favourite subjects and I will answer you in some detail, how much time have we got?'

'You ask an unusual question Zac, do I look like a middle aged Bohemian Artist or at worst an ageing Hippy? Sorry just my little joke, in fact I have no problem with such types, I envy those free spirits. Yes Sarah and I both belong to such an organisation, if you want me to elaborate on any areas you don't understand or are uncertain of please feel free to speak up, okay by you Zac?'

'Yes, Dr Dylen thanks!'

'Our political belief or ideology, is to settle disputes via dialogue, in order to find an alternative way, never by the use of a gun and certainly not by way of a nuclear bomb, that some imbecile had the audacity of mind to invent and then some other fool had clearance from the 'powers to be' to paint the British flag on its nose, to imply the consent of the general public in the United Kingdom.

Society should take a stance over the real dangers towards ordinary people in another country; women and children would certainly be exterminated along with their men folk, whose daily task is to bring food to the table, whole families obliterated without any sense of the humanity. Sorry do I make sense Zac; it's not my intention to talk down to you.'

'I don't mind, you put things to me in such an easy way, I find it quite interesting.'

'If you want an even clearer picture go along to Hyde Park, at the area of Speakers' Corner, on a Sunday morning. It costs nothing to enter and anyone can listen and take on board another's beliefs - at a safe distance. Standing on a wooden crate they will in earnest try to coerce onlookers into their thoughts on a variety of subjects and invite public opinion. Of course, respect must be acknowledged on both sides. For example, refrain from swearing or taking the Queen's name in vain, those are just a few points to remember. The clever public speaker will move into unknown territories about which the passer-by may be unaware. Government policies, taboo subjects such as legalizing homosexuality and abortions plus a variety of other issues. Of course you may not agree with some of those individuals but it gives you an alternative point of view. Go there on a Sunday morning, look, listen and learn and be your own judge on the discussions and enjoy the situation. I think that, at some point in the not-so-distant future, a government may put a stop to such freedom of speech.'

'Have you or Sarah ever stood on a wooden crate and shouted at people?'

'Airing our views loudly in public? No neither Sarah nor I

have taken up the challenge we are listeners rather than speakers, of course some do put on a dramatic show for attention, screaming or shouting to be seen and heard, some rant and rave or just talk gibberish, whereas the clever speaker will be passionate about his beliefs but use logic and wit (oratory/storytelling) to bring attention to themselves.

A good example is Stuart Christie, a Glaswegian, in his early twenties, rather tall and stoops a little, with an appearance of a non-conformist. Long jet-black hair half way down his back, sometimes wears his family tartan. He grew up as an anarchist under the influence of his grandmother; he's written a book you might like to read, it's called 'Granny Made Me an Anarchist.'

Dr. Dylen had my undivided attention, and I nodded to him to continue, then without thinking, interrupted him. 'Excuse me, but what is an anarchist? I've never heard the word before, not even at school.'

"Stuart's definition of anarchism is that it's a movement for social justice through freedom. Anarchism began as it remains today, a direct challenge by the underprivileged against their oppression and exploitation. It opposes both the insidious growth of state power and the ethos of possessive individualism, which ultimately serve only the interests of the few at the expense of the rest.

Anarchism is often seen as a violent force against the government but, as an ideology, it promotes mutual aid, harmony and human solidarity, to achieve a free, classless society. You'd have to read more on the subject, but that's it in a nutshell, if you like.'

'I see what you mean, Dr Dylen, but could I go to Speakers' Corner on my own; are you sure it's safe and I'm not too young?'

'Well, as much as I'd like to take you it's not possible; it would seriously compromise my job. Sorry, Zac, but I'd rather not elaborate further on this subject, perhaps you could go with a friend from the Hostel.'

We check the time as we have to be at the home no later than six o clock, but as conversation is in full flow, we decide to remain.

'My mother lives in Glasgow I wonder if she and Mr. Christie know each other, as they are both Scottish.'

He took his own time before acknowledging my statement.

'I don't really know, he seems a very amenable fellow, if you happen to meet Christie you could ask him yourself, maybe best not to hold on to hope — Glasgow is a big city. Are you curious about your mother?'

'No, not really, but I would like to know more about the young kilt-wearing Scotsman, a dropout sort of character standing on a wooden box on a Sunday morning in in the park, where for fun people are throwing rotten tomatoes at him.'

A long pause, then he turned to look at me, 'For a start Zac, people who bother to attend such meeting of differing minds do not throw, as you say rotten tomatoes or any other sort of missiles at those airing their views at Speakers' Corner. The worst sort of poor manners would be aggressive heckling; so young man, no tomato-throwing as this would amount to hooliganism, I am sure that you are above such acts of bad behaviour, anyhow Zac I can see on your face that you jest with me.'

'Sorry Dr. Dylen.'

'Shall I tell you a true story about Stuart Christie?' I nodded my head in agreement.

'It's not a state secret, it is public knowledge and been reported in every form of media throughout the world. By some means he came to be engaged in an underground movement, for want of a better word, a secret organisation here in London. How he got involved with such people, only he knows. Stuart was really just a youth around seventeen. One has to recognise that he was brought up in a household that had strong political views. Stuart was close to his grandmother and some would say influenced by her ideals, Zac you remember what it means to be an anarchist don't you?'

I paused to recollect what he had just told me! 'I think it means someone who believes in social justice and direct action.'

'Good so let's carry - on where I was.'

'You got to the part when he joined a secret organisation.'

'Yes that's right, now we can't be certain but the consequences of his actions were that he was put into prison to be tried for the attempted assassination of Spain's fascist dictator, General Franco.'

'Was he like our Queen then?'

'Fair comment, but no, that is not a good comparison, the Queen is just a figurehead she shows no outwardly spoken political views but is good for the country in attracting overseas visitors that is about all she does but that is another matter!'

'So how was he caught?'

'According to the press he carried sticks of dynamite under his kilt but I believe this to be a fabrication, a bending of the truth.

Although Stuart Christie freely admitted to playing a part, he crossed the border and went in hiding so to speak, the day before he was to hand over the sticks of gelignite to another member of the secret organisation. An informant sent a message to the dictator's secret police, warning them of the brazen young Scotsman's mission. An old saying I shall offer to you Zac, keep your friends close, but your enemies even closer. The outcome was that Christie was arrested and found guilty by a military court, of trying to kill Europe's last fascist dictator. One has to remember General Franco is a bedfellow, not in the literal term if I may add, of Stalin, Hitler, and Mussolini. If Christie were to be found guilty, it was a foregone conclusion that he would certainly be garroted - are you familiar what that means?'

'Not really,'

'I have to warn you Zechariah, sorry, Zac the next part of my story is fairly gruesome, shall I carry on?'

'If you don't mind' I replied.

'The death penalty in Spain involves fastening a steel collar around the prisoner's neck, then a mechanism with a bolt is thrust into the closure and the collar tightened to inflict a slow and painful death. It is said that General Franco often insists on being present, looking on with pleasure until the victim expires. Sorry it's so gruesome; no doubt Christie may have chosen an alternative plan if he had known what would happen to him.

The outcome was that he was spared the death penalty owing to the attention of the world's media. And to remind you Zac he was only two to three years older than you are now. He was sentenced to a twenty-year imprisonment and spent three-and-a-half years in one of the worst prisons in Spain, in unimaginably filthy conditions at the hands of the dregs of society. Nevertheless, with his height and courage he stayed out of harm's way, eventually learning Spanish and becoming a teacher, helping illiterate Spanish inmates to read and write. When he returned to Britain he was ambushed by the newspaper men of Fleet Street, but he chose to give his story to a newspaper he believed to have acted with integrity. His whereabouts are unknown, but occasionally he still speaks at Hyde Park, providing there are no journalists following him… and that concludes this piece of history regarding the political activist, Mr. Stuart Christie.

Be a good chap and get some more tea and cakes; here's the money and don't forget to ask for a receipt. What a good life to be in a café drinking tea, and getting paid for it into the bargain. Forget I said that Zac, as I mustn't be a bad influence on you! Soon we have to make tracks as we've been here for hours. If I had my way I would stay discussing things but this cannot be. We have an appointment with Captain Frost at the Youth Hostel, at 6 o'clock.

Before we move on, Zac, you're aware that I know your history.'

Putting on his glasses for the first time, he frowned.

'Have you been told about any Neurological issues you may have in addition to your partial deafness?'

My mouth opened wide, my bottom lip drooped. I started to stutter in my reply, saying that I didn't even know what the long word meant, let alone if I indeed had such a thing.

'Please, Dr Dylen, can you explain what you mean?'

He replied, 'Of course I will it's my fault, that's the trouble with people like me, we sometimes forget to use normal words. The word neurological means matters to do with the head, and a slap to the head can affect the brain's wiring system. Do you follow me Zac?'

'Yes I do.'

'That's why your ear plays tricks on you; it's not your fault you know.'

'I suppose I am used to it, but I wonder if that is the reason I have no sense of direction. Mum use to tell me that unless she showed me the way I would be found at a distance walking in any direction. I was brought back home in a police car a few times. She blamed my wanderlust on to 'her' in Scotland and said that she was a wandering Jew and a no-good tramp'.

An awkward silence descended about us and he looked shaken at my last remark.

'Evidence supports a theory that your poor sense of direction may be hereditary. In other words, either your mother or father may have passed it on to you. It's an easy answer but I'm interested in such matters and will see if there is a paper on the subject.'

'Thanks.'

'Zac, do you get bored easily?'

'I suppose I do really, I get fidgety, if you know what I mean. I live in my own world and spend a lot of time in my bedroom from seven o'clock in the evening until the following morning about seven a.m. by which time I am ready for school.'

He leant towards me.' So tell me what do you do to pass the time?'

'Nothing, I just looked out of the loft window, towards the trees across the road.'

'What about reading or listening to the radio, or drawing, perhaps?'

'None of that stuff, Dr Dylen, but I would always kneel beside my bed, looking at the handmade cross given to me by the church at Easter time; then I would count the wallpaper flowers in different ways and lie on my back, with my arms behind me to stop myself fidgeting. I don't mean to be rude, Dr Dylen, but hadn't we better get a move on?'

'Yes, of course, you're right but finally then, why did you go to bed so early? What reason did your parents give you?'

I sighed, as I didn't want to answer any more questions: 'Oh that's easy; it's because when the telly was on I kept asking questions and would fidget so much mum use to tell me I had ants in my pants and was getting on everyone's nerves.'

'How many years do you think your bedtime regime lasted?'

'Let me think, from when mum and dad took me in around four years old, until about eleven years old, when we moved from Bohemia Road to our new house on the West Hill. The Council had given some money for us to move out; our place was to be demolished or something like that.'

He peered over his glasses at me. 'I have to say that none of this was ever recorded on any social workers report. Tell me; were you ever able to talk to one of my colleagues, on a one to one basis?'

'No not that I can remember.'

'And if you were on your own with your social worker, would you have told them about your spent years in the bedroom?'

'Not sure, sorry.' For the first time in my life I was lost for words.

'Let's make a move, Zac, I'm in a bit of a quandary here take my business card and only in case of an emergency, call my office and announce yourself as either Zechariah or Zac from Hastings. Either I or someone I trust will return your call. Remember, this card with my signature is for you alone.

One last point, try to visit Speakers' Corner and if by luck you have the good fortune to meet Stuart Christie tell my first cousin once removed, Sarah and I send Stuart our kind regards.'

As we moved away from the table the young black man came towards us again to collect our dirty dishes, piling them high, ready to be taken away on his trolley. I thanked him again, this time he responded loud and clear: 'Thank you man' I realised that for at least a few hours no customers had even acknowledged his existence!

Dr Dylen and I set off in a London black cab, our destination, the National Home for Boys in South East London. As Victoria Station loomed in the distance, I glanced out of the side window; the fast moving traffic caused a sense of bewilderment and disorientation and of being lost. Dr, Dylen announced 'Five minutes early are better than five late, as Captain Frost is a stickler for punctuality.'

He was at a meeting with Captain Frost only a few days ago, discussing my case and preparing my move to the home. He offered a friendly smile, we shook hands, he bade me farewell and good luck — then reminded me to contact him in an emergency, and to keep his business card in a safe place.

Then he was gone.

AN AFFINITY WITH ANTIQUES

Standing on the pavement outside my new home, I looked up in amazement at the edifice. Purpose-built in 1885, the last quarter of Victoria's reign, to house some of society's disowned, lost or confused youngsters.

I experienced a feeling of déjà vu having seen similar architectural features only a short time before – at the Hastings Museum, built in the style of an Anglo Indian fortress at a time when India was still part of the British Empire, circa 1920. Lord Brassey had bequeathed the building to the people of Hastings. With its hand-carved wall panels, Mehrab style window frames, Mashrabiya turned wood panels inset into original carved decorative window seats and a myriad of many other exemplary features. It was undoubtedly one of Hastings best kept secrets.

Across the road from the Museum is the White Rock Gardens with its abundance of fragrant plants, shrubs, trees and garden seats also a café, several bowling greens, tennis courts and a meteorological station.

During the summer holidays around my eleventh birthday, whilst still living in Bohemia Road before moving over to the West Hill, I used to play on the swings at the White Rock Gardens then when bored, I would cross the road and go to the Museum.

Peering into the glass cabinets my attention was gripped and my curiosity piqued by the coin collection from a bygone age. Who had owned them? What travels had they made? How many wars had they survived?

Throughout the summer holidays excepting Sundays as I had to attend church then I became a regular visitor to the Museum. So much so in fact that the elderly curator took an interest in me, shortly after being informed by another member of staff that I was spending a lot of time there. Thus the curator became aware of my great interest in all old things.

Appreciating my curiosity, the elderly curator would unlock the cabinets and allow me to handle the rare coins. No mention was ever made as to their value. Patiently he passed on his knowledge about how to distinguish important marks, conditions, and how to devise the rare from the mundane.

Over the next few years I would leave my friends on the occasional Saturday afternoon and head up to the Cambridge Road museum.

On my frequent visits a staff member would inform the Curator of my presence, and if available he would come and welcome me. At all times we respected the formalities: I called him by his surname, whilst he referred to me as 'Young Zechariah'.

Staff members and visitors must have thought us a curious sight as we talked earnestly about all manner of objects d'art. Given my inquisitive nature regarding antiques, we moved from coins, china and pottery to paintings and furniture. He would unlock the cabinets and allow me to handle examples of early period porcelain and continental pottery, teaching me how to identify hard and soft paste pottery or porcelain, the use of lead rivets and maker's marks on the base if they existed.

One of his more flamboyant and theatrical demonstrations for testing items for signs of damage would involve holding a valuable and ancient pottery bowl in the air supported by thumb and two fingers, with his other hand he would tap the underside of the vessel in an upward direction to the rim, hoping to hear a high pitched ring. If a flat tone registered, the object either had a hairline crack, or had been through the Porcelain Restorers Workshop. He used the same procedure with glass. Other than this occasional demonstration he was of a reserved nature, a man of the old school.

Patiently he explained the different techniques used in Victorian oil and watercolours, whilst I listened in earnest. He encouraged me to ask questions. I learned how to distinguish original oil paintings from reproductions, 'Oleographs', which were usually German in origin mid to late Victorian in manufacture. A copy of an Old Master or famous painting was printed, lithographically, on a stretched canvas in a Walnut frame. Several coats of a Shellac-based varnish were then applied, 'French polished' and left to dry, after which it was gently brushed with a chemical product to give the appearance of craqueleure 'crazing'. In time the image acquires a veneer, with no clarity or definition — much to the annoyance of discerning collectors and dealers alike.

Another art form popular towards the late nineteenth century was the paper print, in which the picture was overpainted in oils, omitting faces, skies and other fine detail, it was a method to be found usually on small pictures.

The elderly curator favoured early period pen and ink drawings, 19th century Bartollozi sepia prints, book illustrations, religious engravings, and other printing techniques, including Metzotints, Aquatints, Lithographs, Etchings, signed Artists proofs, Woodcuts, and a further source of information regarding paper studies of influence, as seen in old copies of *The Home Lovers Art Book* published by the world-renowned London art gallery, Frost and Reed.

His bias against oil paintings he explained was because mistakes can be covered with the application of several layers of paint, hiding any mistakes, or a change of direction in the way of subject matter. The exception was early sixteenth to eighteenth century religious works of art including Dutch masterpieces; their brush strokes being the signature of an accomplished artist.

His slow pace of mentoring me and his quiet voice captured my attention. One afternoon I mentioned my passion for wood and asked if he would he give me a masterclass on the relative importance of the furniture on display at the Museum. Over the next few years, until I left for London he explained tirelessly how to recognise antique furniture.

I never mentioned my future plans and he never inquired, but he was acutely aware of my lack of academic education and could see I was essentially a hands-on person. His advice was that with my keen interest in antiques, I should pursue a career in furniture restoration as such knowledge and skills were sought after. He could see I had a keen interest, hence his suggestion that I should look for an apprenticeship when I left school.

London was where it was all happening in the 1960s, a city where anything was possible. As the old adage states, it was a case of being in the right place at the right time plus, who you know counts twice as much as what you know.

When assessing the merit of any piece of furniture regardless of age, a keen eye for style is crucial, an often overlooked skill. The cabinetmaker may have an eye for detail, solid construction, quality of timber, and so on but he is often less interested in the finish; this tended to be left to a good finisher, whose talents were often as great as the cabinet maker.

The curators own personal and somewhat negative opinion on the finish of an early piece of furniture was the over-use of French polish in pursuit of a high gloss effect, as opposed to either oil or wax finish. To him this was an abuse of furniture not uncommon in the Victorian and Edwardian period; he opined that eventually shellac would discolour.

Another useful piece of information I picked up concerned veneers of specimen woods, prized for their decorative appeal, that were then glued to an inferior wood such as pine, these were now supplied in thin slices as opposed to the thick hand- or knife-cut veneers of the early period furniture.

He knew I intended eventually to move to London, but was concerned that I was too young to be going alone to the city. I have my reasons, I replied. Nothing more was said on the matter.

Knowing he would be retiring in due course he gave me his collection of back issues of the *Antique Collectors Guide* magazines, as well as his Sotheby's and Christies sales catalogues with their black and white photographs, descriptions and after-sale result sheets. These he said, would be invaluable references for my future studies.

Before parting company he insisted on passing on one final piece of information, 'A marriage,' he said, was a term used by members of the antiques trade and academics, to describe furniture put together with parts that hadn't started their lives together, these were not considered outright fakes but were often a much later deliberate act in order to deceive for financial gain.

'Let that be a lesson to you, young Zechariah', he said as he locked the museum's huge Victorian Gothic arched oak door, for the last time.

We never met again, though I later read with interest in the *Hastings Observer* that he did make it to his retirement with, to quote his last words to me, 'Time to stop and stare — after having dug the garden.'

MY NEW ABODE – CAPTAIN FROST

As I pushed open the tall imposing side gate I was surprised how light it was to the touch, perfectly balanced on its protruding Iron Gate rides. There was a loud buzzing sound as the gate locked behind me. Slowly I walked up the gravel drive clutching my trusty blue hold-all bag which held all my worldly possessions; it seemed to be weighing me down. As I walked up the beech-lined drive I had the uncomfortable feeling I was being watched. On either side of me green and white enamel signs warned people to 'Keep of the Grass'.

A huge timber framed door creaked open and standing in the entrance looking down at me, stood the figure of a short fat man wearing a shirt and tie, a red blazer, grey flannel trousers and gold wire-framed spectacles. He had a sallow complexion, and bore the signs of shaving cuts around his neck and chin.

The man welcomed me with the hint of a West Country accent.

'Zechariah, I presume, perfect punctuality, well done.' He held out his hand, either to welcome me or take my bag. 'My name is Captain Frost.'

We shook hands. 'Now, young man, follow me and shut the door behind you if you please'.

I closed the door with a resounding thump, forgetting to use the polished brass handle. I heard him murmur disapprovingly. This was my first mistake, my face reddened.

'If you don't mind, we prefer to close the door quietly, using the handle'.

I nodded in parrot fashion 'Of course, Captain Frost – sorry.'

Looking at me blankly he said: 'I say old chap, thank you

for addressing me in the correct and respectful manner, no less than I expect. We have rules and standards, I'm sure there will be more issues to iron-out while you are staying with us, now follow me, please'.

Three boys in the hall stood to one side to allow us to pass as we went through to his office. In unison they chirped 'Good afternoon, Captain Frost' while all the time looking me up and down, the eyes telling it all. It was 'I told you so; a new boy was expected today'. I curved one corner of my mouth in a faint smile towards them, but they didn't respond as Captain Frost ushered them on their way.

'This is my office, Zechariah. There are matters I'd like to discuss with you, please take a chair and we'll make a start'.

Captain Frost's shiny balding head showed sparse white stubble. His animated eyes bulged from their sockets in a menacing smile; short stubby fingers indicated he'd never done any serious manual work, and the starched white shirt with its frayed collar and small rust coloured marks was tight around his paunch, almost bursting at the seams.

I was dressed, in my view in the latest anti-establishment fashion of the swinging sixties. A style that didn't go down too well with the older members of our society, who saw us as anti-authoritarian and thus a threat, how dare the youth reject regular short-back-and-sides' haircut, in favour of the Rolling Stones or Beatles look.

His office desk was an imposing large Victorian mahogany knee-hole double pedestal desk, with a racing-green leather top inset and gold-tooled leaf detail around the border, in the Greek key pattern style, with a set of nine drawers to one side with brass swan neck handles.

The room was at least eleven foot high and boasted a

decorative but broken cornice plaster moulding; it retained the original ornate ceiling rose and a wax-polished oak-herringbone pattern parquet floor which stretched into both bay windows, allowing an uninterrupted view of the front garden and entrance gates.

Captain Frost faced me sitting on a brown deep-buttoned leather upholstered swivel chair; I sat on a metal tubular frame plastic stacking chair, one of several around the room. An awkward and uncomfortable silence followed. From the middle drawer he took out a file with my full name on its cover. I couldn't make out the nature of the contents. Speaking quietly, he asked me something I couldn't hear. My lip reading experience was useless as his consonants and vowels weren't clear — he muttered. He repeated the question, this time in a raised voice.

'Again, for the second time, are you sitting comfortably? If so we must make a start as we have the preliminaries to get through and to cover some details.'

I fidgeted, nodding my head a few times.

'Excuse me; did you hear what I just said? Am I talking too quietly or what?' His voice a little tempered

'Yes, I did', I paused '... some of it'.

'Two words you seem to have forgotten to use, you must refer to me at all times as Captain Frost, as the former is the rank I held in the armed forces, the latter of course is my surname, do I make myself clear? I will not allow any form of insubordination from any boy here in my care.'

'Yes, sorry, Captain Frost'.

'Good', he murmured. 'Let's get on with the matter in hand. Your social service report states that at school you were a good timekeeper and well-mannered, cheerful and tidy but, alas without any qualifications, they say you could have done better, also a nice letter from your mother in Hastings sings your praises. So Zechariah, we shall, take each stage bit by bit, and then I can form a clearer idea of your intellect, personality and anything about you.

The cover of my buff-coloured folder bore, in large bold capital letters, the title 'Priory Road, Hastings Secondary School for Boys' followed by my name in neatly written longhand. I shudder to think what this document held regarding my intellectual capacity and foibles. The gist was that I was at the bottom of a stream of seven classes, and among the bottom three out of the standard class of thirty four, as well as being in the bottom stream of seven forms.

When I was twelve, however, and much to my surprise, and everyone else's, I came third to the top of the form. My teachers praised me on my English comprehension and mathematics. They were equally astonished when, the following year, I reverted to my original position among the lowest in the bottom stream. My teachers commented that I had the capacity to acquire an education through repetition, while acknowledging that I was kind and generous towards other pupils. In the classroom however as recalled earlier, I spent most of my time staring out of the window, gazing into space.

At the age of twelve I had a Saturday morning job at an unregistered old people's home on the corner of Bohemia and Church road. The place was home to a small group of around 8 - 10 residents who as far as I was concerned never complained, certainly not in front of me. My mother worked there as a cleaner I am certain she would have had something to say about any abuse. Part of my (poorly remunerated) duties included fetching coal from the cellar, removing the ashes from the old black kitchen range, and then shopping in Hastings town centre. At Woolworth's I would buy broken biscuits by weight, at a reduced price.

On my return Miss Ralph the home's owner would count out four pieces of broken biscuit, which she placed neatly on a saucer, and then taken round on a tray with a cup of tea or diluted juice drink to her paying guests, for their afternoon tea. Miss Ralph was a frugal spinster who, daily and without fail ate boiled fish for her morning breakfast. The smell was dire, I often left the kitchen door ajar and opened the heavy wooden sash window for fresh air. She didn't like me doing this and would wag her finger at me and give me a dressing down. To earn extra pocket money on the run-up to Christmas day, I went around town, knocking on doors, singing carols, trying to sound angelic in my yet unbroken voice. My efforts were usually well-received, especially by the neighbours in and around the local area.

Captain Frost continued 'Remember, the unwise choices you made in your past or in the future will one day be presented before the Almighty. Also do not forget the old adage about the consequence of one's actions. Any questions before we begin? You, after all Zechariah, are the lead role in the pantomime. Please excuse my little joke.'

I smiled, he laughed, showing off his poor dental work of a bygone age.

'Captain Frost, just to let you know I've shortened my name, from Zechariah to Zac. I have decided I need a fresh start with a new name'.

He banged on the desk hard with a clenched fist, his face red and eyes glaring.

'Zac' He shouted, hurting my one functioning right ear.

'What on earth has made you reject Zechariah, the biblical name, from the Old Testament? I thought you were a normal and well-behaved person, not a malfunctioning idiot. You may not be the brightest star in the firmament but why go and say something like that'.

Pausing for breath he continued, 'Are you some form of idiot? Have you been transformed by decadent music, the 'Sixties' cultural revolution, the stupid songs, long cissy-like hair, no respect for your elders? I will remind you that it was people like me, who, only sixteen years ago risked their lives in action to give you your life. Things would have been a lot different under German rule, I can tell you. What is more, I cannot accept the values and ideas of your generation, this so called freedom of speech rubbish.'

I interrupted his flow of abuse by leaning back on the chair causing the thin metal legs to scrape the floor. His voice rose to a high pitch.

'Sit properly, boy. If you have an accident and fall to the floor you could break your back and have to live in a wheelchair for the rest of your life!'

'Sorry. Captain Frost' I said, a flicker of nervousness in my voice. 'Do you mind if we take this a little bit quieter please — my ear hurts, 'I paused.

His chest expanded with a sharp intake of air.

'Of course, I apologize; my outburst was out of order. Please understand I am responsible for so many boys. With such stress on my shoulders my emotions are a little sensitive, although I am concerned about your wanting to change your Christian name. Your mother gave you this name, in Christ's name, so don't you think its bad form to turn your back on it? Anyhow, I won't impose my own biblical thoughts on you. For your benefit though you ought to discuss this with your social worker Dr Dylen.'

'Actually, Captain Frost, the reason I'd like to change my name is, how can I say this, is to rid myself of any attachment to that woman in Scotland. I don't know why she disowned me at birth and should still have any say in my name or upbringing. Dr Dylen has already agreed to my new name, as long as I don't use it for any legal reasons. You can ask him if you don't believe me.'

Silence reigned.

'I believe you Zac and I'm happy for you to call yourself by your new name, I will of course discuss it with Dr Dylen. I'd also like to add Zac, that at some point in the future you should look back at your time in Hastings as a good start in life. It's been so much better than some of the boys living here have had. You seem well-balanced but I recommend you seek some type of help, for example a child welfare expert, who will help get rid of your defence mechanism. Not that I'm an expert on the subject. Like all weaknesses, it needs a little adjustment every now and again. But if you do feel you need a counsellor, I'm sure that between us, Dr Dylen and I will do our utmost to help.'

We shuffled awkwardly in our seats,

'At this point Zac, I suggest we adjourn this meeting for the time being. I'll explain the rules and introduce you to some of the younger boys. How about a nice cup of tea? I'm parched, you must be too. Look! There's Mrs. Tucker, she's just come in for her kitchen duties; let's go downstairs and take some light refreshment. We can continue our chat later, a little less formally I hope. We seem to have aired our different points of view enough for one day. Please collect your bag and follow me.'

I could see that had things been different, when the captain was my age he might have followed a different path, but he had been directed by his peers to a destiny not of his choosing.

We walked along the long narrow hallway, its bare pine floorboards covered with threadbare Persian runners. The canteen was off to the right, down a winding staircase to the basement, tables and chairs were set out informally at angles, to seat around fifteen to twenty boys. A polished stainless-steel shutter filled one side of the room. It was locked to prevent boys stealing packets of crisps to sell on at a profit.

'Mrs. Tucker, I'd like to introduce to you our new full-time boarder Zac. He is fifteen and keen. I would imagine he would like to sample the Friday night fish and chips. Can you accommodate him, have you enough supplies?'

'Of course I'll make sure he has plenty. Sorry, Zac, isn't it? Such a nice name, short for Zechariah of religious origin I seem to remember. My husband's family is from Limerick in Southern Ireland, where that name is very popular.' Her hands opened to me in a gesture of goodwill.

'I think you're right Mrs. Tucker, anyway if there's any problem about tonight's food I'll understand if you're short.'

'Don't be so daft' she smiled, her rosy cheeks shining. 'I'm never that short, don't worry, you are in capable hands here and all the boys call me 'Mrs. T.' or Betty if you prefer. Not too many formalities on my side. The only thing I ask is that, if you know beforehand you won't be here for the evening meal, just let me know. It's such a shame to waste food.' She beamed as she adjusted her headscarf and her chequered chef's cloth cap.

Captain Frost asked 'Could we have two cups of tea then,

or coffee if you prefer? As the boys come down for refreshment I shall introduce you to them one by one. Don't worry about remembering their names in one attempt though. You'll be sharing a bedroom with five boys; I'll ask one of the boys to show you to your dormitory, your new home. Tomorrow, after breakfast, which stops serving at nine forty five sharp, I'll expect to see you in my office directly afterwards, so please be prompt. I have a full schedule planned. We can discuss things such as employment and anything else that may arise. … So, Zac, enjoy your evening'.

Before leaving the canteen Captain Frost introduced me to a small black boy of about 4ft 9. He had short, curly, shiny hair, wide open eyes and a warm welcoming smile. He was the eldest of twins; only thirty minutes separated their births. Just in from school he wore baggy grey flannel short trousers, well below the knee, one size too big; real leather shoes, worn at the heels, his tie hanging out of a pocket, the top two buttons of his shirt undone and a frayed collar. He spoke in an unfamiliar London dialect, but one I could just about understand, as long as I listened carefully.

'Come on man. I show you the way; we are up at the top of the house. What's your name again? The old Captain mentioned it, but I kind of forget it'.

I'm not tall but I towered over him. 'My name is Zac, and you are?' My introduction must have startled him.

'Marco' was his reply.

'Such a cool name, is that for real or what?' I raised my eyebrows indicating a question. There was a brief pause.

'No one here can say my real name, see it's from Africa, at least I think so; my brother tells me so. Anyway, Marco is what I am called.'

His words stopped me in my tracks. It's a good name I replied. 'It's so cool, you have a brother. You are one of twins, yes?'

He swayed his body from side to side. 'My brother's just half an hour older, and not as good at football as me but anyways, he's a cool dude, just like me!'

Now I have his habit of swaying from side to side. 'I'm sure you're right. 'I said

After walking up several flights of stairs we arrived at my shared bedroom, number 4A, my new abode.

'Here we are man, that's your bed by the door; the one next to you on the other side is Johnny's. He's a cool guy, really tall and the bed is too short. One night my brother gets a feather of a squashed pigeon he found in the road and when Johnny was fast asleep, with his feet sticking out the bottom of the bed, he tickled them. Johnny kept on twitching, so funny man; we laughed for hours that night. When you meet my big brother, don't tell him that I told you so, okay man?' He laughed aloud, gyrating at the same time.

'No problem man, I won't say a thing to Johnny. So what's your brother's name? It's not Polo by any chance?' The atmosphere suddenly changed.

'Zac, man, you some sort of spy or someone kind of strange — a witch or something? His name is what you call him.'

'It's just a guess and for your information I know nothing about witchcraft or stupid stuff like that. You see, Marco, I changed a few letters. It makes a lot of sense and it's a good name. Marco Polo's was a real person, an adventurer way back in history. One day I'll tell you about the Explorer, a brave and clever man, I promise, it's cool.'

At that moment his older twin, not quite identical, entered the room. Marco was laughing energetically, hips swaying.

'Polo, this is our new roommate, Zac a really cool man — and he guessed your name and we're both famous.'

In his own way he explained what I'd just said. With the ice broken they spoke in slang about how they might be related to Marco Polo.

'Come on, man, what does Zac mean? I have never heard of such a name.'

'It is short for Zechariah from the bible I think, not as nice as your name.' I was trying to adjust the setting. A common denominator had surfaced, regardless of colour or age. The twins took it in turns helping to unpack my hold all, commenting how neat and tidy my belongings were. I didn't have the heart to tell them my mother had washed and ironed every garment to a high degree with love, care and attention. I soon realised why they were taking such an interest in my belongings, they were clearly looking for anything to which they could help themselves to.

I gave them a couple of cigarettes each, even though they were only nine years old, with me joking that smoking would restrict their growth. A no-smoking sign on the wall seemed not to make any difference whatsoever. Being at the top of the house they said the staff could be seen coming. A lookout was posted on the landing and the youngest bullied into such a task. The one way up was the perfect position as far as security was concerned.

Things had settled down by now and my belongings were stowed away in a grey stove enameled steel cabinet, with two doors but no lock.

Johnny and I warmed to each other immediately; over six

feet tall, lithely-built, with short-cropped hair and high cheek bones. A dimpled chin complemented the killer look.

He dressed like a mod in a bespoke suit, definitely a head-turner of a teenager in his prime, a magnet towards the opposite sex — a man's man with an endearing and warm south London accent. Johnny and I got off to a good start, sharing as we did similar tastes in fashion and music, bantering constantly about the mini-skirted girls on the streets of London at the time.

Adrian was my penultimate roommate. His physical appearance starkly contrasted to mine with his modest, quietly-spoken and self-effacing manner: long jet black hair parted in the centre and a few chin whiskers. He attended the nearby grammar school and was trying for a university scholarship. About 17 years old, he had lived in the home since the age of seven. Well-versed in the arts, his interests ranged from poetry to Russian literature. A fan of Bob Dylan, the Rolling Stones and the Yardbirds, supporting the anti-nuclear disarmament C.N.D. movement and almost as if to prove it at every opportunity he showed off proudly to all and sundry his substantial collection of left-wing badges. He also wore a Che Guevara style beret.

Adrian later told me, in confidence that both his parents had died in a road traffic accident involving their converted de-commissioned Ambulance. Apparently, the motor home driven by his mother was involved in a head on collision with a double decker bus on the outskirts of London; both parents died instantly but Adrian suffered only minor injuries. With no family to take him, he was put into care. During their search of the vehicle the police discovered a large collection of academic books and the parents' university degrees from

Cambridge. Both were apparently outstanding in their chosen fields, and deeply involved in student politics. For some reason Adrian's father had given up his job as a professor of English Classics, sold their possessions and taken to a life on the road where Adrian was educated to a high standard and as a pastime taught to play chess, at which he showed a talent beyond his years.

To reduce tension between the groups and to limit quarrels the dormitory's were divided into full- or part-time boarders, the consensus being that part-timers, with a family support network at weekends and holidays had a tendency to brag obnoxiously, about the large amounts of money spent on them, and regularly ran to Captain Frost with tales of the full-timers shenanigans, which tended to be fabrications and exaggerations. Even Captain Frost showed signs of fatigue and frustration at having to put up with this behaviour.

Simon, who had been in the care system since birth, being moved from one place to another, was the last of our roommates. We knew he was epileptic, though his fits only occurred when stressed, or subjected to flickering or dazzling bright lights. A bewildered wide-eyed stare was usually the signal he was losing control. He had recently had his thirteenth birthday and was still wetting the bed — and talking in his sleep. A quiet, small boy with thick prescription glasses, he was a little too naïve for his own good. A practicing Christian, he was very honest, never smoked, swore or blasphemed, or spoke unkindly about anyone. In fact, when speaking he rarely made eye contact, unless he had no choice in the matter, keeping himself to himself. Unsurprisingly he was a victim of bullies. On the whole the boys left him to his own devices, a lot of the boys called him 'Simple Simon'.

RULES

From Friday night to Monday morning breakfasts and evening meals were served by Mrs. Tucker who regularly offered second helpings. She was often heard to say that we must eat well to grow big and strong, otherwise what's left over would go to waste, well not quite as the local pig farmer would be grateful.

The home had around eleven full-timers, occasionally increasing to about eighteen, so it wasn't unusual for a boy to disappear for some unknown reason. We had the run of the place, particularly the communal recreation room where the volume on the black and white T.V. was always on at high volume and channels were constantly changed, to the annoyance of the older boys.

My window overlooked the back garden where cooking-apple trees stood proud, with limbs clinging to each other for comfort. This was the domain of Jim the gardener, who wielded his razor-sharp loppers to sever each limb in quick succession. Jim's passion was for root vegetables. On more than one occasion I saw him from my window hiding contraband vegetables under his oversize jumper. A Londoner, a loner and a poor communicator, although in fairness perhaps he felt it best to keep his distance from us; it wasn't unusual for boys to spread unfounded rumours about the character of those employed by the National Home for Boys. It often caused otherwise worthwhile individuals to seek alternative work elsewhere.

Any boy found telling tales to the Captain was sent to Coventry (the silent treatment) for up to one month, depending on the crime. For the younger boys there were threats of violence and name-calling, a snitch or a grass or worse. It may have been harsh but we had our own rules. On more than one occasion if one of us was being picked on albeit by a street gang or bullied within the home, the older ones would try to reason with the offender. If this failed the silent treatment would follow. Only the knife-carrying gang on the landing below relied on violence, although I should add that for some unknown reason, never once did they threaten us on landing four.

One occasion Johnny, Adrian, and I, along with five boys from the knife gang discovered that the twins, Marco and Polo, were being bullied and racially-abused by an older boy at school. The 11-year-old offender was with his mother and sister and two female friends outside the school gates when we approached them. Their startled faces displayed their humiliation. We had decided beforehand that Adrian, being the most diplomatic and well-balanced would speak for the twins.

As the smaller children gathered around us it became clear that the spiteful boy's mother was involved with a black man. She had recently started a new relationship after her divorce and was 'living in sin' as they used to call it. She claimed to be ashamed of her son's racist behaviour which she had been aware of, and told her son not to take out his problems on the twins.

Her two teenage daughters clearly smitten with Johnny's good looks giggled and fluttered their eye-lashes. Clearly they had taken a shine to him and his friends, all of which helped defuse the situation. Adrian ignored their larking about and continued stating the case on the twin's behalf while the older members of our gang happily showed off in front of the girls.

The boy's mother addressed her wayward son, asking him

what he'd do if a close family member or friend was lying injured or dying in the road and only person around was a black doctor. She told us her son would be dealt with, it would be her number one priority, and that he would apologise to the twins for the upset he had caused, adding that if she ever discovered him picking on innocent children again she would punish him unhesitatingly in a way he would never forget.

The boy shook hands with the twins and the matter was resolved. Then, with a smile, the mother told her two daughters to follow her home at once, giving us a sideways glance over her shoulder, telling her daughters in a loud voice to leave those naughty boys alone, there was too many to choose from anyway. With that we all roared with laughter, common sense having finally prevailed and an altercation prevented.

INTERRUPTED SLEEP

My first night at the home was unnerving; there was so much grunting, snoring, movements in and out of the bathroom and in the early morning. Simon's nocturnal activities opposite me; his blankets moving and the final sigh of sexual relief. I had to turn to the wall in embarrassment.

I wore pyjamas, Johnny pyjama bottoms and a T shirt, Adrian likewise, but with a CND logo on his T shirt. The twins slept in their underpants and Simon completely naked.

The night duty manager, Captain Frost's deputy was a former lieutenant in the British Army, a disciplinarian of few words. We were, without exception, in fear of him. At every opportunity he would repeat his mantra: 'I say what I mean and I mean what I say.'

We all agreed however, that like the Captain and his wife who went out of her way to care for the young children in the home; all three staff members were fair and generous with their time.

My best friend worked at Saville Row. He had a five-year apprenticeship for world-renowned tailors to the Queen. He often boasted how one day he would make his own suits for the rich and famous. We were kindred spirits he said, and that he would show me around London.

On Sunday afternoons a group of us would head off, after the midday prayer meeting to cause havoc in pursuit of girls and have fun in Petticoat Lane market. The only exception was Adrian, who most Sundays, either went to Speakers' Corner in Hyde Park, or remained indoors with his studies, taking advantage of the Sabbath peace and quiet.

On one occasion I went to Speakers' Corner with Adrian, but it wasn't a place I would consider going on my own; I got lost very easily, my mind would go blank and I would get disoriented.

'Good morning. Captain Frost', I announced as I entered the room at the appointed time that first Friday.

'Come in, Zac, I trust you have settled into your new home? I hope that by now you have met your room mates and that they made you feel welcome. Was the bed comfortable, and are you are enjoying your new surroundings? Have you enjoyed Mrs. Tucker's hearty breakfast? She takes great care in her cooking and is proud of her culinary skills'.

'Yes thank you everything is alright Captain Frost.'

He nodded, 'Right let's move on to the topic of employment; as you know you are of working age and it's only right and proper that you are in work. Idle hands makes the Devil's day, if you know what I mean. Anyway, an income from you is what's needed. At your age you can't expect to live off charity.'

His eyes fixed on mine.

'No of course not, I would like to work and pay for my keep.'

He smiled, displaying his stained teeth.

'Good Zac, we understand one another and are singing from the same hymn sheet. Where shall I start? Yes, I know, at 10.30 this morning you have an interview for a job in a cheese factory near London Bridge station. Everything is arranged, I have connections you see.'

He smiled 'Your first job in the cheese factory has good prospects Zac, if you play your cards right. That's what the young say isn't it, play your cards right? The phrase is almost poetic, don't you think?'

'Of course Captain Frost exactly so, out of curiosity is it

good money?'

'My dear boy, of course and it has a future to take care of your development. I think they employ around three hundred staff. It'll be your first job on the employment ladder; you'll be part of a team on a conveyor belt, filling tins of cheese to the brim ready for consumption.'

'Sounds good Captain Frost, my only problem is finding the place. I don't know London; I reckon it's a lot bigger than Hastings.'

'My dear boy, your small community in Hastings would fit into London a hundred times over at least and that's on the conservative side. I'll draw a map for you, it's the least I can do, it's my job one I hold dear to my heart. I'm here on behalf of the 'Home' to help all the boys in my care.

THE FACTORY, TOOLEY STREET, LONDON BRIDGE.

On the first Monday of October 1965, an autumn morning, I found myself on my way to my first ever employment interview at a cheese factory. As I strolled down the hill to the tube station with London born-and-bred Johnny, whom I knew for certain I could trust, I confessed to him my abysmal sense of direction. At first he laughed in disbelief then, taking me seriously, he wrote down the directions to and from my place of future employment from where he would leave me most mornings.

I could have travelled with him, had we left at the same time but he had to leave much earlier than I, often working an eleven hour day. It would have been too great an imposition to expect him to accompany me as I wanted to be able to fend for myself. Was this long day's toil normal in London for a 15-year old, or was it the exception I asked myself.

The interview went well and I got the job, starting the next day at eight thirty. The interviewer was an ordinary-looking, middle-aged man who I believed to be a close friend of Captain Frost and his wife. After the interview a straightforward journey took me to a coffee bar near Tower Bridge station where 'The Who' was playing on the jukebox. I felt a tremendous sense of freedom. Afterwards I made my way back to the home without too much difficulty, praising myself that I was becoming street-wise and to tell Captain Frost my welcome news.

It was a five-day working week, from Monday to Friday and if required Saturday morning too, at overtime rates of time-and-a-quarter for the first four hours, thereafter time-and-a-half. This seemed to be standard employment practice at the time.

Captain Frost reiterated his belief I had landed myself a splendid job and that if I kept my head down, worked hard, I'd soon be a respectable tax-paying British citizen. I would then be in a position to get married, have children, buy a house and a car, all by the age of twenty two.

The wage for a standard forty-hour week was twelve pounds seventeen shillings and sixpence, minus deductions and tube fairs, which meant I would be left with around ten pounds out of which I had to pay a quarter of my income for my keep at the home.

As Captain Frost said, those with an income should help finance those less fortunate.

I had to work a week in hand so getting through eleven days including weekends was difficult. Johnny offered me a loan and the Captain also offered his help, which I declined. I still had some funds which, as long as I stopped smoking less and stayed in over the weekend, would just about allow me to manage the situation. It also gave me the chance to get used to my new abode, meet other boarders and work at being accepted.

It was surprising how many of us had little or no money. The youngest had just enough to purchase a few sweets, nothing more. Clothes were hand-me-downs from charity shops or seconds from large clothing stores but socks, underpants and shoes were new so they said, as were school uniforms.

My payment towards my keep was four pounds a week, twelve pounds divided by three. I got lucky however, as my first wage slip showed an amount of nine pounds. This was due to having only worked the Tuesday to Friday that first week. In effect I was left with three pounds twelve and sixpence per week; all my overtime pay I could keep for myself. I was on to a good thing, especially living in London.

Betty was aware of my circumstances; every breakfast time gave me a small parcel of food and a soft drink to get me through the day and to make me not feel out of place among my work colleagues at break times. She also made sure I had a substantial meal and her undivided attention in the evening. Her kindness continued until I received my first week's wage. Little did she know how much she had saved me? Having to sit without food in the company of my workmates would have been highly embarrassing. As time passed however, my colleagues, mostly Black, Asian, Irish and Londoners of all ages, became aware of my situation at the 'Home' and they certainly wouldn't have seen me go hungry.

I was the youngest white boy in the factory. The work involved standing at a long conveyor belt, handling scorching-hot tins that burnt my fingertips, the tins having only just emerged from a high temperature industrial oven to erase bacteria. All the men on the factory floor wore white overalls and cloth caps, the women wore hairnets.

In the background the radio blared out popular songs from Radio Caroline, music from an illegal decommissioned ship moored just outside British waters in the English Channel, away from the clutches of the British government authorities. The sound of loud music, with young and old singing cheerfully out of tune to songs such as Chain Gang, an American Negro song, about those held in ankle chains while wielding a sledge hammer breaking rocks as punishment for their black skin.

Conversation was kept to a minimum because of the noisy

steel rollers. So, with funnels of cheese filling up the cans to the correct amount, any bottleneck due to inattention would bring the factory to an abrupt standstill and lead to a verbal warning. Three warnings and you were dismissed, those were the rules. Fortunately I was quick -witted and this never happened to me; the gossipers caused these holdups. Although our charge-hand was Paddy, a huge big-bellied, rosy-cheeked Irishman, who overlooked such matters, his report usually, stated the fault lay with the machine, not the employee.

I enjoyed the work but the heat of the tins on my bare hands did cause me considerable discomfort, as did standing in one position for long hours.

I was ecstatic when at lunchtime on Friday my first week's wage packet was handed to me in a brown, sealed envelope. The feel of the notes and the clinking of the coins were exciting for me to handle. Also, it was an early day for us; we finished at four-fifteen on a Friday afternoon which meant we could avoid the rush-hour.

I handed my unopened wage packet to the Captain who said; from that day forth it would be for me to open the packet at my leisure. Friday evening or Saturday morning would be time enough for him to receive my board and lodging, of the sum of three pounds per week. Unwittingly, he calculated the amount in my favour by not allowing for the fact that my first pay packet was for four days worked, while a normal week was five days.

I knew I was fiddling and my guilt led me to confide in Johnny who shrugged his shoulders reassuring me that it wasn't outright theft; I was just bending a rule. Rules, he said, were made to be broken and anyone in my position would have done the same. He reminded me that I was completely on my own in London, with no parents or family members to rely on, cigarettes, discos, girls, travel and clothing all have to be paid for by whatever means possible.

PYJAMAS ALL ROUND

With my first week's wages burning a hole in my pocket and it being a Saturday afternoon, I decided to visit the local street market with Johnny, the twins and Simon who didn't really want to come for fear of being attacked by local youths roaming the streets. I reassured him that no harm would come to him as he was in safe hands and good company, although I wasn't a particularly good fighter.

By way of temptation I told him I had a treat for him at the local coffee bar. The burgers and soft drinks were on me, and there was another treat. Adrian however offered me some invaluable advice, which was everyone at the home, apart from the weekend boarders, would look upon my kindness as a form of weakness. Their inbuilt defence mechanisms would soon kick in, so beware of that captivating smile.

Simon and I chatted away as we headed towards the underground, although it was a bit of a one-sided conversation since he was inclined to offer only monosyllabic answers. I felt uncomfortable in his presence, perhaps he wasn't used to being in a one-to-one conversation, though only small talk was involved. This may have been owing to the chaos of living with the constant shouting, screaming, and occasional confrontations, especially among the younger boys, that often ended in a brawl. Having any in-depth conversation in the home was difficult with so many interruptions, No matter where you tried to find a quiet corner someone would find you and make life difficult.

The twins giggled and were showing off, holding my attention; they were little blighters in their own right.

At the market we found a stall selling exactly what I was looking for. My new-found friends the twins, chose their first-ever pyjamas, dancing in front of the black woman stallholder who made sure they had the right sizes. I encouraged Simon to pick out a pair for himself also.

Simon stood to one side, alone, with tears rolling down his cheeks and mucous pouring from each nostril. I rested my hand on his shoulder as he sobbed uncontrollably. Fortunately the twins were too involved in their antics to take notice. He explained, chokingly, he only ever had hand-me-down pyjamas. A few years earlier he said some of the other boys spat at him, and they made him wear girls' pyjamas with a teddy-bear pattern and called him a queer.

The stallholder guessed we were from the home and offered me a small discount, remarking how polite and well behaved we all were. Then, without warning, she came round to our side of the stall and gave the twins a huge hug, burying their tiny heads deep in her bosom. Wrapping our purchases and commenting on our 'please and thank you', she gave me an unexpected discount. A bonus was the five smiling and beaming faces.

We then moved on to a local coffee bar for hamburgers and drinks, where Johnny paid for the jukebox, each of us choosing our favourite songs. We passed a group of boys but they offered no trouble, some of them knew Johnny from school, so just stares and grunts.

A few weeks passed without problem, and indeed I was happy and felt at home at the house. Even the short forty-five minute religious ceremony and tuneless singing of hymns in the kitchen gave me a sense of well-being, also I was happy at work and I got on well with the majority of my multi-cultural work colleagues.

Mondays to Fridays I wouldn't go out in the evenings. The

sitting room, whose focal point was a huge marble, rouge-veined fireplace surround, had three large distressed sofas placed strategically around the walls. Captain Frost knew we smoked and there was no lower age restriction on this, he had the common sense to know he could not win on that one. Older boys who smoked their Players' Navy Cut cigarette, down to the filter, would throw ends, still lit, across the room to one of several under ten year olds for a drag. They would catch the cigarettes with both hands, and pass it on to one another. These fag-ends looked disgusting with soggy spittle and tooth-marks.

There were usually arguments over television programs until lights out at nine-thirty pm. The younger ones would hide to avoid going to bed. Their soft brittle worn out toothbrushes were kept collectively, I refused to leave mine with the others, keeping my own toothbrush in its cellophane wrapper in the top drawer of the bedside cabinet by my bed. I advised Johnny, Adrian, and Simon to do likewise given the likelihood of the spread of gum disease. They took my advice and after much badgering the twins did likewise, albeit they concluded that because they were related they could share a single brush, for the time being. One day I bought different coloured brushes for Simon, Marco, and Polo all of different colours and brushing their teeth became a fun thing for them to do.

Owing to a spate of thefts, Johnny suggested I ask the Captain if I could keep my spare cash and documents in a jiffy bag in the safe. It was a good idea. If ever I needed access the Captain and his wife were usually around, as was his deputy Mr. Hughes, who also had a key and the combination to the huge steel safe.

Johnny was courting a 15-year old girl at the time; he had

met her on a lunch break whilst delivering a suit to a rich business man at an office in Regent Street. Carol was a temporary assistant whose duties' included delivering parcels and letters to the Post Office, making tea, coffee, and general go for this, that, and any other menial job a junior would be asked to carry out. He took her to coffee bars, cinemas and by tube across London to her home in Penge. She had to be home by no later than ten-thirty and if lucky Johnny would steal a kiss or two and try to touch her breasts, only to be rebuked with a sharp slap on the wrist, followed by the remark that she was too young. Carol didn't want to be known as a girl of easy virtue.

'You're a fast worker, but I'm a good girl, so behave yourself you bad boy. You'll have to wait till I get to know you better'.

Of course that could mean anything, depending on the girl's moral values and her sexual appetite, if she had any.

On Saturday evenings I would walk down the hill to our favourite coffee bar with the twins, Simon and some of the older boys. We may have looked like a gang looking for trouble, but we weren't. On one occasion we were taunted and jeered at by another group of lads but nothing came of it as our boy's home had a reputation for being tough. A few years previously there had been a street fight and a few of our older boys had badly injured the leader of another gang. They were charged with Actual Bodily Harm (ABH) and each sentenced to Borstal for three years, so the story goes. We, however, were more interested in popular music, fashion, and chasing after mini-skirted girls.

I wasn't aware of any obvious racism, though an undercurrent of racism lurked in the air. The music industry helped improve the situation. I recall once in the coffee bar a lad commenting on the colour of a black boy's skin when the would-be victim commented: 'If you don't like the colour of my skin then why do you spend the money in the jukebox, choosing Wilson Pickett, the Supremes' so on and so forth. Answer this one to me man, for your information they are all black.'

The aggressor's bottom lip drooped and that was the end of that situation. A clear message I thought, but there was many a word spoken between us that an outsider might have regarded as racist. Much depended on who you were talking to, the tone of voice and the look in the eye. We had a common interest in not hurting each other's feelings; the attitude was 'If you dish it out you must also be able to take it'.

Calling each other names helped to break down barriers.

One afternoon at work just as the siren signaled the return to work, a serious fight broke out between a large black woman and an equally robust Irish woman; they worked on the same conveyor belt. Screaming and shouting and cursing at each other, the two women began pushing each other on the factory floor.

'He only wants you when your knickers are off. We all know you're a whore.'

The other retaliated, 'You bitch. Get back to your own country'.

Violence escalated as they grabbed handfuls of the other's hair, kicked, biting and drawing blood as they wrestled grotesquely on the floor. The fight continued for a rather too-long five minutes, before Paddy our charge-hand, and a small bespectacled-manager tried in vain to split them up. Paddy restrained the Irish woman, but the small manager was unable to hold back the black woman, so I shot across to help. Although not of athletic build, I am wiry and fast and managed to pull the woman away. In the scuffle, however, a fist hit me in the eye and my vision started to blur, I didn't feel any pain at the time. Eventually other men intervened, the women were separated and the situation calmed down.

I soon had an enormous black eye, the shiner of all shiners, the pain was excruciating. Both women were fired on the spot, neither of whom had been in any trouble previously. They were punctual, clean and reliable timekeepers, both with young children and had worked for the company for around five years. I felt sorry for them. According to gossip the women lived in the same high-rise flats and shared time together even walking to work, seemingly the same husband to.

Seeing I was in pain I was taken up to managers' offices two floors up, where the head of the office junior from Accounts sent for water and a clean white linen towel. As the girl bathed my eye she told me she'd had first-aid training and that her mum was a nurse. With my one good eye I recognised her at once. I had often noticed her on the shop floor and on the tube. How fortuitous that she should be my 'lady with the lamp'.

She administered first aid, under the watchful eyes of the older women, all of whom were passing comments about the obvious flirting between us.

My bad eye began to feel better under the girl's soothing touch. I grunted and groaned as my cunning mind worked overtime, playing for sympathy. I was hoping she'd keep up her attention until clocking- off time.

The manager asked if I wanted hospital treatment and

stated that the injury must be logged and registered. I declined the offer of hospital treatment, but readily accepted the offer of a paid taxi home with someone accompanying me. I asked cheekily, if my pretty, ministering-angel could come with me, a request to which the company agreed.

A London black cab picked us up from the front door, where a charge hand signed the time card authorization, ensuring that I would be paid for the rest of the working day. My ministering- angel was salaried and, being a clerical worker, didn't need to clock on or off. In the taxi with my leather coat by my side I chatted away to her, trying to make eye contact with my one good eye, not the best flirtatious move I've ever made. She asked my name and if I was alright, showing genuine concern.

'Aye, aye, captain.' I said jokingly. 'No, my eye really does hurt ... Anyway; you know my name, what's yours? I can't call your Florence Nightingale can I?'

She chuckled teasingly. 'Judy Finnegan ... and don't you dare ask where Punch is or I'll give you another black eye, then you'll have a pair Zac okay.'

'I wouldn't have dreamed of asking where Punch was, whoops slip of the tongue, silly me. I'd better make it up to you Judy. How about my treat, I take you to the cinema next Saturday night, or has some other fella got lucky? If you're free perhaps you could look on me with a little pity. My eye hurts so much ... if only I was being cared for by, what's her name, yes I know Judy that pretty girl from the factory, oh my eye hurts'.

'Don't play the poor, soft boy with me, Zac. You shouldn't get involved in women's fights; in case they turn on you. Anyway, I haven't got a fella at the moment, so if you want to take me to the cinema that's okay but remember Zac, I'm a good Irish girl so don't be expecting any hanky-panky in the back row and another thing I'll be paying for myself, okay. I'm earning as well, best you know it.'

'Good idea, Judy not the back row, fair enough. How about second-to-the-back instead? By the way, I'm scared of the dark so you'd best hold my hand.'

My usual ability to be witty and frivolous wasn't up to scratch, largely due to the bruising and pain in my eye.

'So now, mother of God, you want me to hold your hand Zac? I think I'm going to have trouble with you, so I'll be wearing my worst perfume, that's for sure.'

'Don't wear any' I paused

'Zac, you are asking me not to wear any what? You never finished your sentence and don't you dare say what I think you're thinking.'

'Oh, sorry, it's come to me now; wait a moment, it's my brain playing tricks, where was I? Yes, I remember, next Saturday night you are not going to wear, now what's the word I'm looking for…?'

'Zac, the word you're looking for is perfume, not something else. I really will have to keep an eye on you.'

We both laughed good-humorously for the rest of the journey in which she took the lead by holding my hand, without any embarrassment. When we arrived at my address, two grandiose large semi-detached Victorian houses knocked into one, with an entrance gate and intercom. She and the taxi driver were dumbfounded.

'Is this the right address, mate?' the taxi driver inquired.

'Yes, sure is. Thanks, can you wait a moment while I say goodbye to my friend.'

'Will do, chum, you carry on.'

'Cheers mate.'

'Do you really live here in that large house, Zac who are you, is it your parents' house?'

'No, not quite, Judy it's a children's home.'

'Is it an orphanage?'

'Well I wouldn't quite put it that way, but kind of I suppose. It's a National Home for Boys from seven to eighteen and we aren't here because we have been in trouble, we are not bad people, Judy. Most of us on our own wouldn't harm a fly. Are you ashamed at being here?'

'No, of course not, I just feel sad. You seem so normal.'

'I am normal Judy, no horns sticking out of my head… Sorry, just joking, but can we talk about this another time, please. By the way, I have a confession to make. I've seen you on the tube going backwards and forwards to work and I think you're really pretty. There, I've said what I wanted to say, will you still come out with me next Saturday evening or does this change things? It's up to you, but I will understand and still want to be your friend.' She reached over and kissed me gently on the lips.

'See you Monday morning on the tube, as usual and I hope your shiner gets better, so be off with you before I start to cry.'

I got out of the cab and waved Judy goodbye. At the home everyone believed I was a fighter of sorts, because of my monster black eye; it gave me street-cred of which I was proud.

On the tube, on my way to work, I noticed the way that people avoided making eye contact with me. It was macabre. What would their reaction have been if I had been a female victim of domestic abuse? I'd probably have been treated like someone with leprosy. That's the reason why so many of society's victims, young and old alike prefer to be left alone, taking refuge behind closed doors. At work people treated me with kid gloves. The only one I wanted concern from was Judy; who was by this time my girlfriend. The older women especially gossiped about how happy the young lovebirds looked.

That first Saturday night I travelled by tube, all spruced up with a hip brand-new, polo neck Shetland wool jumper. The twins Marco and Polo both wished me luck, although they were a little jealous; I usually spent Saturdays with them. Things change, however; I was on a journey from boyhood to maturity, but I think they understood.

I met Judy outside the tube station where we caught the bus to the cinema at Marble Arch. The choice of film was hers. It was a 'U' title, indicating its suitability for the under sixteens, but what the film was I can't remember. Judy's outfit was stunning, white knee-length boots with platform soles, a stylish 'Biba' top and the shortest of mini-skirts imaginable, showing off her gorgeous legs.

I was smitten. Her blue eyes with black eyelashes, Mary Quant hairstyle, natural fair hair and just enough make-up on to awaken my sexual desire. Arm-in-arm, with our full-length mod leather coats we were the picture of fashion-conscious teenagers. We removed our coats and headed for the back row. Other couples began to fill the vacant seats but I've no doubt most of the males there weren't interested in the film. Like myself we all had ulterior motives, as did, maybe, the girls, it was after all 1965. The lights dimmed and on came 'Pathé News' with its crowing cockerel. I had no interest in the news so, stretching my arm along the top of the adjoining seat, I slid my hand around her right shoulder. She showed no sign of resistance and moved closer. My imagination was going wild at the thought of her miniskirt rising to reveal her luscious, sexy thighs and legs.

When the film started, my right hand started to move slowly towards her pert breasts. God, how I wanted to caress them; my mind was in overdrive. She gently pushed my hand away, but not aggressively. Choosing not to press the matter further, I just slipped my hand into hers.

After about 45 minutes we started to kiss, full-on on the lips. It was closed mouths but it was a start. Judy obviously didn't feel uncomfortable given that most of the couples around us were involved in some form or another of heavy petting.

Until that point I had dated at least half a dozen girlfriends in Hastings, but the furthest I had been with a girl was touching inside her knickers, and for her to do likewise, making me ejaculate. Going all the way however was not an option, or we would face an unwanted pregnancy.

'My mum and dad want to see you, so you're invited over tomorrow afternoon. We can go to the park at Camberwell Green after and then on to my favourite coffee bar, play some records. What you think?'

She gave me her most flattering look, a habit acquired from a very young age and practiced regularly on her father. Thus was I drawn into her spider's web.

Adrian drew a map for me on the condition that I accompany him to Speakers' Corner one Sunday afternoon. I agreed and indicated the following week would be perfect, weather permitting. For some reason he only wanted either mine or Johnny's company, certainly no girls.

Work was going well. There were no problems and I felt

good. I was becoming increasingly thrifty, saving the three pounds from the National Home for Boys lodgings that I was able to fiddle. It went straight into the Captain's safe, nice and secure for me to put to good use one-day. I was still not going out during the week, although Judy had hinted that a Wednesday evening out would be nice. I resisted the temptation, not wanting to start something I might want to stop at some time. I enjoyed being with the youngsters at the home, their hilarity and the mischievous behaviour they got up to. I was met at the bus stop close to the main road at Camberwell Green, where the bus diverts to another route. Adrian's map was correct in every detail, with the names printed in longhand for me to recognise the landmarks. I managed to get on the right bus on the right side of the road and sat near to the conductor who said he would give me the nod when it was my stop.

My stop was the one after the Camberwell School of Arts, where Judy was waiting for me, with a hug and a kiss. I felt obliged to drop my macho guard and confess to her that I wasn't blessed with a functioning sense of direction.

I asked a few of the women on the conveyor-belt about meeting my girlfriend's parents for the first time. They promptly passed on my request down the line of around thirty women, during the break they openly discussed in front of me, what they would bring to Judy's parents by way of a gift. The suggestions ranged from a packet of 'Durex' to a box of chocolates; the most popular was a bouquet of flowers. Most of them agreed that it was the woman of the household who had the biggest say in such matters, although if the husband smoked, ciggies would also be welcomed.

I explained to the women jurors that my pocket couldn't

extend as far as tobacco on top of the flowers, an admission they found funny. They made good-natured jokes that I'd be likely to hand over an unopened wage packet, in return for their daughter's hand in marriage. 'The wife knows best' they chanted, so hand over the wages for safekeeping. They had a point: children had to be clothed, watered and fed and, whatever their colour or religion, offspring always came first. I wondered why my birth mother hadn't shared these views. I hold such women in high esteem, and wish I could understand the no-hoper women in society.

As Judy and I walked along the road, she surprised me with yet another outfit. How did she do it? I was still wearing the previous night's clothes, except clean underwear and socks.

As we approached a large Victorian house she told me her mother and father had moved there from the Elephant and Castle area. They were now buying the apartment on a mortgage basis. She was proud of the fact that after two years they had broken away from the council high-rise flat. Her mum worked as a nurse in a Paddington hospital, while her dad now worked as a doorman in a private club in Soho's Green Street, checking clients credentials and for the most part, deterring the unruly or the inebriated from entering the establishment.

I was a little nervous but with Judy by my side what could go wrong? I had bought a new pair of socks the previous day recommended by the women at work, given that it was customary to remove one's shoes on going in the front door, which I duly did. Brenda, Judy's mum ushered us into the front room, the best room, taking the flowers I offered, commenting graciously on the fragrant bouquet. She was a nice looking woman with the accent of a lark singing in the early morning. Like mother like daughter I thought.

Waiting in the best room was Judy's dad, Seamus, a short stockily-built close-shaven-headed man with huge arms, the like of which I'd never seen before. I thought he was a Londoner, but it turned out he was southern Irish but had lost the gentle, harmonious, accent. Seamus sat in his armchair, indicating me to come forward and to hush. A race at Goodwood was under starter's orders and he had a good pile on the horse's nose to win. I sat listening, watching the occasional horse dismounting its rider or another wretched horse falling at a fence and ending up on its back, unable to get up. It was the first time I had seen such a horse race and witnessed the extreme force of the jockeys' whips beating the sides of the poor animals. I concluded that if man had to cause such pain to an innocent creature to acquire wealth then I was graced by Gods to have my job at the Tooley Street factory. At least I could sleep at night in the knowledge I had done an honest day's work for an honest day's pay.

All I could hear from Judy's father was, 'Hit him harder, faster, faster!' and other expletives which I have to say I felt uncomfortable with. To cap it all once the race was over, he took one look at me with my shoulder-length hair and said: 'Don't you think you ought to get a haircut. What on earth does your mother think of you, are you a cissy or what? Oh, sorry, silly me, I forgot, your mother's not around is she… that's why you live at that home, that orphanage with all of those other misfits. Never mind, leave it to me. I'll sort you out in no time, just wait-and-see.'

'Thank you, Mr. Milligan for inviting me to tea', I said blushing.

'Well, well I have to admit you got some manners. I reckon the National Home for Boys must have taught you some. Zac come here boy, let me show you my boxing trophies, see them up on the mantelpiece? Do you box; can you stand your own? I reckon you're a light- to middleweight am I right? Come on, own up.'

At that moment Judy and Brenda came into the room providing a welcome interruption and for a few hours we all sat in the front room. Seamus insisted that the television was kept on as he wanted to see a particular programme, although the volume was turned down. He had a knack of interjecting small talk into the conversation every so often while keeping an eye on the TV screen.

When we were about to leave for Judy and her mother to attend Mass at the nearby Catholic Church - I had been coerced, somewhat reluctantly, into going - Seamus said he wanted to show me one of his boxing medals. Judy and Brenda were to remain on the landing as it was man's talk. I followed him back into the hallway, removing my shoes again, and passed through into the living room. He stood by the fireplace surround, and squared me up in a very confrontational manner.

'Now this won't take long boy, this is strictly between you and me. What I am going to say I mean, and I mean what I say, got it or do I have to spell it out? Listen and listen well. First, you are not I repeat not, going to touch my daughter in a way that I do not feel is appropriate, we are talking sex, in case you don't understand me, don't under estimate me, ok? Listen, orphan- or bastard boy, whatever you prefer. I will put it another way, keep your filthy hands off my daughter. I don't want the likes of you being in her company, she is too good for you.'

Slapping me hard on the right cheek, he gave a menacing

smile: 'Good, you got the message, now be off with you, and by the way, have a nice time.'

Back in the hall I put on my shoes and made my way downstairs to the lobby, where Judy and Brenda were waiting.

'What happened to your face, Zac?' Brenda asked. 'It's all red, under your black eye.'

'It just came out red. I don't know why. Maybe it's a reaction from me rubbing it.'

'Well, Zac, if it happens again, you really must see a doctor. I've never seen or heard anything like that before. If you want I could make an arrangement for you to see the duty practitioner at the hospital where I work. Judy could take you there if you want.'

'No thanks, Mrs. Milligan; it's probably just one of those things. I've rubbed it too hard, or something.'

'Judy, keep monitoring his eye, he needs someone to watch over him. It'll be no problem at the hospital; there are a lot of good doctors there.'

'Okay, mum, will do. Now come on, Zac, I just don't know what to do with you.'

Taking my arm without hesitation, the three of us set off for the church, which was about a quarter of a mile away. In the fresh air, my reddened cheek returned to normal, but with Judy's father's outburst I was feeling a little apprehensive, even walking by Judy's side, to say nothing about any future possible intimacy.

The Catholic Church was nice; I especially liked the singing, the friendly handshakes and listening to Judy and Brenda in fine voice, then watching them making the sign of the cross and kissing their rosaries. I wondered why Seamus didn't come with us, it certainly would have made him a much better-tempered person and able to deal with his inner-demons. Judy and I had planned on an evening out after the service, under the pretext of an unexpected meeting with Captain Frost; I made my excuses and said I had to leave. Judy and her mother walked me to the right bus stop, and waited until the bus came along and I was safely on board.

I felt a keen sense of relief. Even if I were a mean street fighter, which I'm not, unless provoked to snapping point, I was in no way a match for her father. I didn't fancy being beaten to a pulp, not even for Judy's sake.

Much as I liked Judy I kept my distance in fear of her father for the next couple of weeks. When we did go out and hold hands I felt distinctly cowardly and deceitful. I had to find a way of breaking up with her, but doing so without hurting her feelings. I fantasized about eloping to 'Gretna Green', but I had a nasty feeling that Seamus might have an army of thugs at his disposal that would find me and do me serious injury. Being the coward that I am, I didn't fancy that option.

Over the next few weeks I fell back on ridiculous girly stories, such as washing my hair. I felt so angry that Judy's father should have such a negative impact on our lives. I hated him with a hatred that ate into my soul but I would never divulge the truth to Judy about the incident with her father. By what right did he have such a say in my life, let alone Judy's life? The only reason I could think of was that he was an angry and frustrated animal, with my apologies to the animal kingdom.

As girls confided in each other, I had Johnny to advise me.

'To get over one girl, you have to get over (and on top of) another.'

That was his simplistic reasoning, and I could see the point, so I stood Judy up. I imagined her waiting to meet me at the pre-arranged bus stop. How long she waited I don't know. Even if she had tried to find a working phone box in the area, she still couldn't have contacted me; residents weren't allowed incoming or outgoing phone calls.

Johnny, meanwhile, had arranged a blind date for me; it was the sister of the girl he was seeing over in Penge.

PENGE

The girl was about sixteen or so, and up for fun and a laugh I hoped. It was the blind-date situation; I was off to meet another girl, Elaine. On the bus Johnny showed me a packet of three condoms, we laughed about how we could share them out, two into three obviously was an unsolvable dilemma. The bus driver had heard us and was smirking.

On arrival at Penge, I was introduced to Johnny's girl Carol, Elaine and their mother, Ruth; the girls were very attractive. The father had left the family a year or two earlier, he returned at weekends when possible to try to re-engage with the family but to no avail. Ruth wanted to be free from humiliation, to which her husband had reduced her. Anyway the girls were now in the era of mid-1960 and with their mother mentoring them they were determined to make something of themselves.

Their mother was working all hours at a bar where her choice of male company was foreboding. Carol the eldest daughter, with her welcoming smile was making her way up the retail trade's ladder; one's heart melted in her presence. She knew life's game plan, a jungle and she knew how to play it. She was an expert and put this down to guessing or surmising others' thoughts, no doubt about it. Elaine, my blind date admitted an insatiably curiosity. I asked her to express this in simple language, to which she replied that she was an inquirer of the mind. Eventually she would like to become a journalist; we all have stories to be dissected, examined and her journalistic skill could be sold to the highest bidder. Money makes the world revolve, forget the rest. Intellectually Elaine was beyond me at the outset; I did find her mind attractive, more than the physical side of her.

I was still thinking of Judy; hoping she that she wasn't still waiting at the bus stop. It's at least one hour since the time of that date. Johnny and I were to go upstairs to the sisters' double bedroom. I knew Johnny had been there before. He had admitted this and told me; in great detail how Carol had allowed him to fondle her breasts for a considerable time by his standards. She then let him use his fingers in search of the hidden treasure inside her panties, returning the compliment by touching his erect penis from the outside of his jeans. For the time being that was to be the limit of her sexual explorations; in her own words she wasn't going to be the local bike. Meanwhile, Elaine and I hit it off straightaway. The chemistry had taken its hold.

The large bedroom held two single beds, eight feet apart; the vinyl blue Dansette machine playing at full blast, a little crackly owing to the worn out needle. Both girls' stashed their clothes out of view in a single wardrobe, the oak-veneered plywood dressing-table, flanked by drawers either side of the tall adjustable mirror adorned with a huge variety of lipsticks, and the usual assortment of girlie make up. It was a clean comfortable room, with posters of the Beatles, the Hollies, and The Who, sellotaped to mauve hand-painted walls. Things were scattered around in a chaotic manner. Johnny and Carol held each other in an embrace, someone suggested we turn off the main lamp to create an ambience; both Johnny and I were lulling the sisters into a sense of security and calm, so that we could seduce them along our way of thinking, our quest to have our touchy-feely way with them. I knew that they had confided with each other and pointed out to us that the light reflected under the closed door from the landing, could be seen by their mother.

Anyway, their mother would be going to her bed soon, her

room was situated at the end of the hallway next to the toilet-come-bathroom. By this time it was around nine-thirty in the evening. A knock on the bedroom door, a couple of gentle taps, then, at Carol's invitation, Ruth came in. The girls swung their legs over the edge of the bed, while Johnny and I sat beside them, with a look of embarrassment about our blushing faces.

'I am just going to bed; do you know what time it is? Are you boys not going to be missed by your guardians? Out here in Penge the last tube leaves at ten-fifteen, otherwise you'll have to take the night bus and cut across the city, but beware, as those buses are dangerous, as well you know. There are still some of those Teddy boys and Spivs in gangs, always on the lookout for a fight, so be careful now. Try not to make too much noise, and please don't keep on playing the same record, over and over again. Anyway, I'm off to bed, and girls make sure that you lock and bolt the front door after your friends have left, good night and be good, I'm placing my trust in you'.

Pointing to her daughters, at which each one gave their mother a hug, and whispers were exchanged, my ear was playing tricks with me, but in any case I was unable to hear what they said.

Johnny smiled at me with a look of victory. I whispered to him that, even if we left now, my guess was we'd be at least half-an-hour late for our Saturday night curfew of eleven o'clock.

Johnny had arranged a cunning plan beforehand in the event of us being late arriving back home, the twins were instructed to make both our beds look as if they had been slept in, and to keep the sash windows ajar on the ground floor so that when the main gate was unlocked in the morning at eight-thirty, we could slip downstairs into the kitchen area.

Boys caught staying out all night was an unknown entity, as was the penalty. We had no intentions of abandoning our pubescent adventure. Our sexual well-being couldn't be held at bay with testosterone levels riding so high; the girls libido was at boiling point, I could tell that Elaine though sixteen coming on seventeen, and myself fifteen nearly sixteen that she was far ahead of me in terms of sexual maturity. The main room light was switched off; Johnny and Carol although not quite in her bed were tearing the clothes off each other in an overwhelming sense of lust. I assumed they had previously done a lot of petting; this time regardless of the lack of privacy, the sexual urge had no bounds.

Meanwhile, I was heavy-petting with Elaine. I had never had intercourse before and made the mistake of stopping after I had my hand inside her thin cotton bra, my other hand clumsily trying to undo the clasp on the back. As I did the vinyl record slipped, I fumbled in the dark trying to restart the music, but the needle arm overshot the outside edge of the LP with a high-pitched scratching. Elaine jumped out of bed, angry with me for defacing her favourite L.P., adjusting herself back into a normal state of dress. I apologised and whispered to her that I would buy her a new one. She put on another record telling me not unkindly, that from now on she was in charge of the record player but if I wanted to later on, I may choose the music from her collection of L.P.s, - her pride and joy.

With the momentum lost we lay on the single bed, kissing and whispering a little. Eventually I slowly went back to my formal position with my hand up her jumper. This time she took the initiative and removed her bra, it dropped to the floor. Her short skirt was riding high; my hand was between her legs just above her knees. Opening her legs obligingly, my hand moved between her thighs and we kissed, our tongues searching for each other. I slowly slid down and licked her breast; her nipples swollen, standing erect, sensitive to the touch. She placed her hand between my legs around my thighs, as I slowly moved my hand up towards her panties.

Once I had reached inside her panties with her legs apart, she at the same time touched the furthest point between my legs. I put my index finger up the side and around the front of her panties while she unzipped my jeans. Every move I made was in sync with her; without undoing my belt she put her hand outside of my pants and took grip of my erection. At the same time my index finger found its way past her few pubic hairs into her waiting slit, she was wet with desire.

Slowly I put my finger to the limit into her; she was panting heavily; my finger was now pushing up and down. Undoing my belt, she put her hand straight down the front of my pants her hand now with a light grip, masturbating me to such an extent that I came all over her hand. Then she went into a spasm, stiffened and suddenly groaned rather loudly with delight. In a tender loving way we lay there, my arms around her she soon turned over and dropped off into a deep sleep. I covered us both with the top blanket, purely for modesty's sake. I am sure Johnny and Carol were awake throughout, listening to the heavenly sounds of our sexual initiation.

THE MORNING AFTER THE NIGHT BEFORE.

At seven-thirty-five on a fine autumn morning, having travelled by tube and bus, we were in a state of non-stop talk, exchanging an abundance of expletives. Johnny and I were in a state of euphoria. We arranged to meet the sisters the following Friday night; we walked at an earnest pace, past the Queen Elizabeth Hospital towards the Home, giggling and laughing.

My voice, having just begun to break, had that squeaky kind of menacing tone, which from Johnny's angle was making him prod and pull funny faces, as he tried to imitate my high-pitched speech; his voice had broken by his fourteenth birthday so he said. He put the sudden change in my voice down to my recent sexual encounters with Elaine, and reminded me that, after sex my voice would remain altered and pitched high. I would talk like that for the rest of my life; of course I believed him, thinking I was to be punished after sex, and my freakish voice would always be a reminder of my first sexual encounter, where the girl in question showed her gratitude and released her inhibitions to me, although no intercourse had taken place.

The open window on the ground floor was in view; the plan was to enter the building with stealth and calm. The large sash window creaked and groaned under Johnny's exertions. We climbed in, scuffing the knees of our Wrangler jeans, falling headfirst onto the wooden floor. The bedroom contained six beds, the steel-framed type, cold and intimidating. Three boys, all around the ages of twelve coming on thirteen, were to my surprise sitting up in bed — our welcoming party. My voice, croaking in its comical fashion, made the boys giggle and laugh out loud, one of them said that we were for it now and that everyone at the home had known of our behaviour towards the Captain's Saturday night curfew.

Both Johnny and I were nonchalant, hanging on to our sense of rightness. We opened the bedroom door and turned left up the flight of stairs trying to avoid the squeaks and groans of the old wooden staircase. At the top of the stairs with Johnny right behind me, I opened the painted white-panelled pine door. A sudden shock hit us; sitting on each of our beds, a couple of suited, stern-looking men around forty years of age, with a non-descriptive character about them. They were holding their badge of authority, the insignia leather bound shield of her Majesty's police force. We were nabbed with nowhere to go. I could see my fellow roommates sitting on their beds, dumbfounded by the course of events. I knew very well that my group of room friends wouldn't willingly have offered any information to the Captain, who had a duty to inform the local constabulary. So it must have been by way of the chattering between the boys below stairs, who by menace or ignorance had given the game away. The Police officers duly marched us handcuffs wrist-to-wrist side-by-side downstairs to Captain Frost's office, the room just off the hallway on the ground floor.

'I say, is this really necessary, for heaven's sake,' he exclaimed. 'These two lads are not even sixteen yet. Surely there's no need to apprehend them in such a manner.'

The captain, on leaving the armed forces worked for years as a missionary in the darkest continents around the world — stood there in a fully pristine pressed suit, looking every bit the person of authority that he was.

The grim-faced blond plainclothes policeman remonstrated

with the old captain, his hand and my hand rising up and down, performing like some synchronized modern ballet. I was used to his gesturing, so I let my wrist go all limp, as to not show any form of resistance.

'It's a matter of procedure to handcuff these types of boys. We are all too familiar with these little bastards; they are a public nuisance. It's well-known that most of these boys sooner or later end up in prison. They have to be cuffed to prevent them running away or resisting arrest. This boy in particular' he said pointing to Johnny 'has the glint in his eye of the most vicious character in the making.'

'How can you say such a thing, I know them both well. At most they could be accused of high spirits, and especially Zac, a little non-conformist. Other than his long hair and the remains of the bruising to his eye, which wasn't his fault, I have never encountered any evidence of errant behaviour in his character. And I should add that Johnny is doing so well as an apprentice tailor at Saville Row. If he is to be charged with some criminal offence how would his employers take it? He would be instantly dismissed and unemployable. I only called you as it was my duty. These youngsters are in my care, and when it came to my attention that their beds had not been slept in I had had no option. I wish I have dealt with this matter internally then get to the bottom of the matter.

Now look at the situation. You are insisting they go down to the police station for questioning, handcuffed to you two police officers'.

The captain was going red in the face, his face in a state of alarm and despair.

'Just doing our job sir, so if you please we will be on our way. Thank you Captain Frost for contacting us, it was the right thing to do. I bid you good morning'.

'Yes' his blood pressure level had risen to boiling point. 'I bid both of you a good day, though I would like you at all times to keep me informed as to their whereabouts. I understand you have an official crime reference number, so let me have this at your earliest convenience.'

We were led to an unmarked police car, Johnny and I handcuffed together on the back seat, told not to make a sound and that whatever we said would be given in evidence, and so on and so forth. For the moment I was a little disoriented. As we drove through the London streets on that quiet Sunday morning I started to hyperventilate; it felt like being on a fairground attraction with everything whizzing before my eyes.

Johnny and I made no small talk; at most he raised his eyebrows, a frown of curiosity about the situation he found himself in. On arrival we were led up the steps to the front of Camberwell police station, a familiar sight, I had been past many times before. We were still handcuffed to each other; Johnny's wrist is left to my right, and with my captor having his hand to the small of my back acting in an authoritative manner.

'And what have we here?' said the tall, lanky, duty sergeant. 'What are your names date of birth and places of residence?'

'My name is Johnny Lee Evans, I am fifteen years old and I live at the National Home for boys at …South London.'

"Good, but I did ask for your date of birth boy. I guess you did have some sort of mother didn't you." He smirked, the officers by our side chuckling with delight.

'Oh yes, twenty-ninth of January nineteen-forty-nine.' Johnny never flinched.

'Your turn now son, so your name is? I reckon I'd better slow down, as you sure don't look quite the ticket. So come on, let's be having it and don't dare lie to me or it's the cat-of-nine-tails for you.'

With this the three of them and a couple more officers who by now were grouped around us started to laugh at our expense.

'My name is Zac Cohen, born on the twenty seventh of April nineteen-forty-nine and I live at the same address as Johnny,' I pointed with my only other freehand.

'Now boy, I will say this, you are an irreverent liar. Look dimwit, I know you are not Zac so for the last time what is your real name, the one given to you by your mother who used to work in Soho — a night worker if you get my meaning.' With this last remark the men by now were falling about with laughter and making lewd remarks, such as, the oldest whore of all whores working in the red light district.

I didn't get the joke and only remember seeing Johnny look at me earnestly. 'Sorry, my name is Zechariah Cohen. I don't like that name so I call myself Zac.' Johnny gazed at me and turned away.

'That's exactly the name I've got here written down in front of me, that didn't hurt now did it? See you can tell the truth can't you?' He looked over to officers behind us.

'Take these two reprobates or should I say bastards, I mean prisoners, down to the cells, remove their belts, shoes, empty their pockets and put them in separate cells.'

We were led downstairs to the basement area; our handcuffs removed and escorted by one custody officer, a big, burly and not so unfriendly man, who used our Christian names. He even called me Zac, asking us if we would like water, maybe tea or coffee later, and asked if we were on drugs or some form of medication. He appeared quite concerned, telling us not to worry, it was just procedure and to use the assistance button if we had any queries or worries.

It was around nine-fifty a.m., on a late November morning and aged fifteen that I found myself in a Police-prison, awaiting questioning about my friend and our whereabouts that Saturday evening. I could smell the disinfectant used to mask the stench of the previous occupants' alcohol abuse and the smell of urine. The cell contained a single-plank wooden bed bolted to the concrete floor by steel plates, a slop bucket in the corner, five sheets of toilet paper and a steel door with a small oblong window for the guards to check on us at their leisure. The fluorescent lighting, harsh and undimmable was protected by a steel mesh frame. I lay on the bed, outstretched, head spinning, my mind doing somersaults...

'Zac, you alright mate?' Johnny was calling to me from next-door.

Suddenly a deep voice from one of the other cells next to Johnny's shouted slurred obscenities, and what he would like to do with us given half a chance. Johnny and I stopped speaking; we had clearly awakened the drunk from his sleep.

After a few hours we were taken separately to a sparsely-furnished CID office, where we were questioned by three stern-faced officers. I was asked to account for my whereabouts the previous night, with names and addresses and so on. I told them the truth, Johnny and I had stayed with the girls in their bedroom listening to music, but omitting the sexual shenanigans that went about. I respected Elaine's privacy and in any case I couldn't understand what business it was of theirs?

First they accused us of house burglary, warehouse theft and shoplifting; although they had to admit no contraband was found on me. Eventually, after taking my statement and reading it back to me, they adjourned the interrogation and offered us some refreshments. This I took eagerly; I was so hungry, and it had been hours since I had eaten, the night before. After tea and sandwiches they resumed their questioning, still insisting on an address, but as my knowledge of London was almost zero I couldn't offer them this. They got my notes, history and medical records and seemed a little perturbed.

After the passage of time a woman entered the room; someone whom I thought was probably from Social Services. With a softly spoken voice she advised me that, if I wished, I did not have to answer any more questions. In an authoritive manner she told the senior officer that they had overstepped the judicial line of inquiry; I was under sixteen, still classified as a minor and that at all times I should have an independent person, either parent or guardian at my side. She also suggested in Johnny's case although he was not in her charge, the case would be in the public interest and that on his request she would act as an independent adult, and offer him her support.

I thanked her for coming. She was from Dr Dylan's Department; he was furious about the chain of events and was demanding a copy of the notes, ever since I had been detained at the Home early on Sunday morning.

I recognised the seriousness of my action, and was informed that Johnny, in an adjacent room, stated an almost verbatim account as mine of the events of that Saturday night and Sunday morning with the girls. Johnny had also added their address, how he had first met Carol and where she lived. To my surprise, after they compared notes with other officers, the conclusion was we would shortly be released and driven back to the Home. To my alarm however, they were going to pursue their lines of inquiry with Carol, and Elaine also their mother and possibly press formal charges of sexual indecency by the two girls towards us two boys; as they were over the ages of sixteen, the charge maybe underage sexual cohesion, or at worst rape of juveniles.

I sat down, saying in a most polite way, that nothing of the sort had occurred and that it was an untrue charge towards the sisters. They advised me to be silent and that the lesser charge of a lewd act with minors could be admissible. I held my ground insisting that no physical contact had been made and that we had just listened to LP's accompanied by general chitchat. Fortunately, Johnny, who was standing by the side of one of the officers, heard every word I said. He signed a written statement, admitting to her in front of the Police officers including myself, that his literary skills were not forthcoming but he understood the charge, he suffered from word blindness also he could not read or write. At this the woman became adamant and stood her ground and again reminded the officers that we were allowed legal aid to be represented and that due to Johnny's distress she should be entrusted and allowed to read his statement through to the end, while in the presence of the police officers. She was escorted to a small room with Johnny by her side and allowed to read the verbal account of events written up by one of the policemen. In attendance was a uniformed officer at the doorway, as these proceedings were most unusual to say the least.

She read his version of accounts, which were to entirely true except for a few misconceptions about the nature of the way it was construed, and that the only discriminating evidence towards the situation, was the unopened packet of 'Durex', found on Johnny, which he readily admitted to owning, that it was intended as a joke to show the boys back at the home. He said that he bought them as he was only six to seven weeks away from his sixteenth birthday, and that 'boys will be boys.' Some spelling mistakes and innuendos in this statement had come to her attention, and that leanings towards fabrication were evident, especially as in her words our client had little understanding of the written word.

By now hostility was rising towards our adviser. Initials altered the statement, and some words extracted to assist both parties. The police stated that in due course, that the only line of inquiry, if at all, would be to clarify the girls address, and that, providing our alibi was confirmed, we would be allowed to go home and if need be sent in a patrol car, with a female officer present.

The offer was declined, not in any unfriendly manner; my social worker said she would take the matter in hand herself. She thought it right and proper to discuss the matter with Captain Frost regarding the recent events. On release I observed the change of attitude towards the each of us. The officers in turn wished us well and handed to Jonny details about part time evening classes at a college that he might think of turning his attention to and that our employers would not be informed of our misdemeanors and the matter was now closed.

On our way back I chatted with her, noticing how casually-dressed she was for the position she held. Her name Miss

Olivia Loveridge told me she was Dr Dylen's niece, and that her father was a Government Human Rights minister, dedicated to the fair and equal treatment of people.

Back at the Home, Johnny and I thanked our benefactor, saying we would take notice of our altercation with the police and the outcome, also her role in getting us out of the cells. Wishing her good luck, she gave us both a hug which was unexpected and clumsily reciprocated. The three of us laughed in embarrassment, tainted with a feeling of warmth, security and foreboding, she then went to have a word with Captain Frost in private to explain what had happened and to be lenient with us. In her words we were young and with the changing attitudes towards the youth of nineteen-sixty-five, things were to evolve in a dramatic way; like our adult guardians, we were on a voyage of discovery, as they had also in their past lives.

I was indebted to the Captain for his insight and compassion over our situation. Acting on instinct he had contacted my social worker, Dr Dylen, who in turn contacted his niece Olivia Loveridge given her legal knowledge regarding the treatment of juveniles in police custody.

Betty, our canteen cook, gave us both a huge slap-up breakfast. We were both tired and looking for some respite, sleep hopefully, to clear away the memory of the police station and our uncomfortable cells. After the canteen had been cleared we thought it only right and proper to attend the church service and to thank his holiness. This was a religious ceremony that occurred every Sunday morning. Only a few boys ever attended the service, maybe out of pity for the Captain and his wife.

Captain Frost was pleased that we had taken part in the

religious gathering; with hymn books at the ready and that we had played down our recent adventure to other boarders who were keen to find out about our escapades and the workings of Camberwell police station.

The next day I had a bad guilt feeling of empathy toward Judy, whom I had let down, by failing to meet her at the bus stop at the agreed time. Was she my Achilles Heel? My attention reverted to her father, behind his facade however, he was a selfish brute of a man who was stealing her sense of fun. Judy and I had become friends, though she and I knew this was a false state of affairs, and there were questions to be answered.

Johnny and I were close but not in a familiar way. Homosexual feelings can surface between kindred spirits in a way that can enhance the inquiring mind and such juvenile emotions. Johnny was getting on well at Saville Row, while I myself took a step up the career ladder and headed for the accounts department. I don't know if Judy spoke on my behalf to someone of influence in accounts on the next floor up in the factory floor. I neither interrogated her, nor used my natural charm to find out.

My savings were growing; my smoking habit had reduced to ten a day, though I probably gave my mates at the hostel ciggies a-plenty throughout the week, as was usual. I became close to Adrian, who was two years older than me. As I listened to him I hung on his every word of wisdom and became interested in the CND movement. He told me of his future aspirations of becoming an anthologist in which he went into detail explaining to me what it was

In another room on the landing beneath ours was Nigel the leader of a gang, a Dickensian character in style, encouraged seven-to-nine-year-old boys to become his small-time thieves at the local shops, in particular Woolworth's store. With his gang he would engage a young Saturday girl assistant in conversation to divert attention, while his band of three or four light fingered small children would help themselves to the goods on display. The assistant knew the boys were thieving, if security was around they would scarper, running in all directions, a tactic known as doing the splits. At the end of their shift of petty thieving, they would all meet up to be almost strip-searched by the gang leaders.

On one occasion a boy of about ten concealed a packet of sweets down his pants. What was a common sight he kept touching his genitals, either as a matter of habit or of urgency? When he had done wrong, some minor misbehavior for which he would ask for forgiveness. It was common for him to offer the offended person a feel of his private parts or to masturbate older boys. One such occasion was an incident in the communal kitchen area, being heavy-handed and clumsy he accidentally spilt a glass of milk on the table. Betty reprimanded him, throwing him a tea cloth to wipe the table; with this he cowered in a defensive position and was about to unzip his trousers. Betty was extremely embarrassed at his proposal and ignored his unusual behavior. On another occasion the boy was caught by his gang members for stealing from them and was made to expose himself by standing at a bus stop on the busy Peckham Rye Lane Road, during the rush-hour, where several buses had to slow down owing to him causing traffic congestion.

A month or so later he disappeared. Rumour had it that he had been committed to a secure unit for his own safety; it was also hearsay that his punishment turned to pleasure, as he was often seen masturbating at the windows of the home when females of all sizes and ages passed by.

The ritual of washing our own clothes was that until you became of working age, or at least if you had money of your own, all clothing was washed en-masse once a week in a huge industrial machine. Unless you had your name sewn into the garment's it was a free for all, underwear worn by others. Johnny and I gave Adrian cash so he could join us in the recently-opened Launderette, where we had great fun meeting mothers with their daughters. The girls were shy and embarrassed at our obvious delight at seeing their bras and panties.

Our fun manifested itself in a cunning way, flirting behind the girls' mothers' backs, a game all teenagers enjoy. Some of the mothers tried to take us under their wing, showing us how to press creases in jeans, an offer we declined as we told them our trousers went under the mattress, folded in a particular way to form the perfect trouser crease. Such silly boys they murmured and tutted, they must be from that Children's home up the road. We, on the other hand, would chuckle and scurry away hand in hand with their teenage daughters, smiling provocatively at our outrageous behaviour.

Occasionally we would meet up with girls from the launderette and lighten the dark crisp winter's evenings with light-hearted kissing and touching in a shop doorway, out of sight of the general public.

The full-time boarders were an elitist group of boys; with no break from each other at weekends, we assumed a responsibility towards each other. The exception was Marvin; he occupied a dormitory opposite to ours and was both a general nuisance and an outrageous liar, exceeding even the stories of Marco Polo. His fantasies knew no bounds, but he was generous to a fault with his ciggies and sweets. His affluent parents lived on Highgate Hill in North London home life was shared with an older brother and younger sister. His mother was a social worker and a probation officer, his father a deputy headmaster in the Westminster area of London. It was rumoured it was his parents' second marriage.

Marvin was tall, fair-haired, pale complexion with good teeth and of the utmost cleanliness including his personal habits.

It became clear that Marvin had strange habits however. His jacket, once placed in position, would have to remain at the exact spot. Even if moved slightly he would demand to know quite aggressively who had moved it; occasionally he would threaten violence. His aggressive behaviour was the reason he had been placed in the home and sent to a special school. On Fridays after a week in the special school he stayed with his parents until Sunday.

My freedom was paramount and I had no intention of holding back or restricting myself in any way. I was my own first priority. Johnny was an exception; he often submitted himself to a life after work, and sometimes went his own way at weekends. He answered to no one; this last ideal had been deeply embedded in our psyche at the National Home for Boys. Go right, go left, or straight on, we were responsible for our own decisions, a selfless act made one stronger to assist through even the darkest and most treacherous paths that lay ahead. If I slipped on a banana skin in the middle of a busy thoroughfare, people may laugh at that moment but the moment is just that, soon it is all past history.

Time was passing without too many incidents. As promised

I called Mum regularly in Hastings, every three to four weeks or so and kept to a regular routine. She was happy and concerned about my well-being. She also kept me up-dated on the family goings on at home. Judy and I kept our distance. I was pleased to see her with a new boyfriend but in my heart I felt she was on the rebound, my behaviour towards her remained respectful. I wondered, did her father slap her new boyfriend's cheek too, as he had done to me, or was he no threat to his manhood? I wished them well but didn't go so far as to tell them this. I still longed to kiss her pretty face, touch her blonde hair and to behold her kindness.

THE TIME OF LOWEST EBB

One weekend afternoon, a Saturday, I am certain of this for the day in question impressed me deeply as to how unkind people can be. Johnny and I travelled by bus to a South-East London suburb.

It wasn't a particularly affluent area, with ragged and unkempt-looking children playing in the street. Nevertheless, I wasn't there as a critic or a voyeur merely observing the behaviour of others in the ever-changing class structure of 1965 Britain.

With Johnny I was in safe company; he was versed in cockney-rhyming-slang, some of which he passed on to me. Living at the home had given him a solid base and his future work prospects were looking good. Walking up to the large block of high-rise flats past folks' kitchen windows and front doors, we were overwhelmed by the shouting, and slamming of doors with children within screaming for attention.

At the end of the landing, Johnny knocked and banged menacingly on the door, commenting that the bell was out of order when his family took over the flat, the council's promise to mend it had never materialised.

We were at his former home, as this was his birthday. On festive occasions he visited his mother and would learn about his brothers and sisters, never knowing how many there would be, their ages, even their existence. They were separated into different homes. As far as he was aware he was the eldest of, at a guess, five other siblings who were scattered like confetti around London.

His foot had now taken over from his fist pounding the door. Nearby was group of small children playing Hopscotch? One a boy who looked about seven to nine, long hair, and a runny nose managed consistently by his cuff-sleeve, informed us that she was at home and had a man from a faraway land staying there. Black as coal, black as the ace of spades, were the remarks in Cockney slang, in unison from the gang of five, who had no idea why we happened to be on the doorstep.

Two of the small boys were teasing one of the other girls, in harmony singing 'She Loves You', by 'The Beatles', their small fingers pointing in Johnny's direction; such innocent fun. The door was suddenly thrown wide open, so hard in fact that its hinges creaked and groaned at the speed and force, the handle hitting a piece of furniture in its wake. Standing in the door frame was a huge black man the likes of which I had never encountered. Dressed only in an off-white string vest and Y-front pants he was sweating profusely, staring down at us in an alarming way. 'Who the hell are you two? What's going on, can't you see I'm busy?'

'I've come to see my mum', Johnny's voice trembled with fear, his face ashen.

A woman's voice in the background asked what all the commotion was about; calling him back to bed to finish what he had started. My eyes diverted to his sagging pants which bore witness to a dwindling erection.

'Mum, it's me, Johnny. Just came over to see you, got my best pal with me, Zac, You can meet him if you want'. He stopped in mid-sentence, turning his eyes towards mine, picking up on my gaze towards the big black American's crutch.

'Johnny, another time, after Christmas in the New Year, can't you see I'm busy, now go away before I lose my bloody temper. Carl, come back to bed. My son meant no harm; I need you, it's urgent.'

The door slammed hard, its heavy frame buckling under the velocity of the violence. The group of children had witnessed this scene, causing the two little girls to cry aloud, making things worse. The boys were saying menacing things, like he's coming to get you after dark and so on. We turned on our heels, not a word spoken, until we were out of the tenement building onto the large frontage. Suddenly, Johnny stopped in his tracks as if struck by a bolt of lightning. He began shouting 'Whore, whore, whore of the worst kind.' His ranting was interrupted only by tears flooding down onto his newly pressed shirt, worn for that special occasion. He was so ashamed of humiliation as he put it to me, that I was to promise never to tell anyone about the incident. I've never actually said a word to anyone, certainly not to the boys back home. He told me a popular saying among teenage boys: The five f's: find them, feel them, finger them, fuck them and then forget them.

I was influenced by the studious Adrian, the oldest boy left at the home, including part-time boarders. He must have been about seventeen. His manner was gentle and passive, his advice given freely to those seeking to widen their horizons. Non-judgmental, gossip never interested him, nor did he indulge in it. He was my mentor.

Adrian was taking his A-Levels at a college not far from Camberwell, and enjoying the relatively new practice of sharing a classroom with the opposite sex, which he found enlightening; before then the sexes had been kept quite separate. Adrian never spoke in a derogatory way about girls; only once he remarked that the voice of Joni Mitchell and Joan Baez's lyrics gave him great pleasure and joy. My taste in female singers was the feminine Sandie Shaw, and the resonant

Dionne Warwick. For some the music world came down to a choice between the Beatles and the Rolling Stones. I preferred the former.

Adrian recognised my thirst for learning and that with his help I would find my destiny. On the plus side I was happy, contented and self-assured about living and working independently, far from my Hastings home as a fifteen-year-old in London.

My best subjects were basic Maths, English and a poor third, geography. Adrian was optimistic that by diligence and hard work I would get sufficient decent grades to get me a place at a teachers' training college. My intention was to become a primary school teacher. I had, in the past thought that such a vocation helping the young to a good start in life would be and spiritually rewarding; the best start in life is to be educated and self-assured in and around all sorts of people, from the humblest to the wealthiest.

So a plan was hatched. After Christmas, advised by Adrian, I would buy easy-learning books, to give me a start in pursuit of a career that I felt comfortable with. With my accommodation secure, I could stay at the hostel until my eighteenth birthday due to studying; even though I was working as well. I was serious and started frequenting the local library. Under Adrian's influence I read books such as *White Fang* by Jack London, *On the Road* by Jack Kerouac - anything that captured my imagination. I was a voracious reader, but not of the pseudo-intellectual kind. I knew my room-mates and companions were important to me, not to be ignored now I had a new friend, the written word on the page.

Since the altercation with his mother and her lover, Johnny was subdued and moody, behaving in a way that made me sad and worried about his well-being. He began considering giving up his poorly-paid apprenticeship as a cloth-cutter at a tailors in a prestigious Royal warrant-holding company in London's Saville Row. What better credentials could he have had? At the end of five years training he would be a fully-paid member of staff, with a fine salary and a bright future. We had long and deep discussions as to whether or not he should resign for the sake of higher wages as a general labourer on a building site with a new group of teenagers who he often mixed with. He finally decided in favour of higher wages, that and the fact that his new friends had found him a bedsit, sharing with them.

He was sixteen, which meant he had a say in his future. Giving the Captain just a week's notice after nine years, he finally walked out of the gates of the National Home for Boys at the end of December. He thanked me for our friendship and hoped that we would meet up again; joking that I would make a good school teacher and that if he had children he would like them to attend my class. He reminded me of my saying to him, give me a child from nought to the age of seven and I will give you the person; the formative years in any child's life are of the utmost importance.

The bed next to mine was now empty, its steel locker vacant. The feeling inside me darkened my soul. The only ones left were a nervous Simon the bed-wetter, the twins and me to watch over my young friends.

TAKING THE LEAD

Johnny's departure left a deep hole, so much so that one night Marco was to be heard sobbing while Polo was grunting loudly. I moved over to his bed, not turning on the adjustable overhead reading lamp for fear of waking Simon and others. Sitting on the edge of the bed I talked to the young Polo who was having problems at school. I would try to take care of the matter. Polo said that Johnny's absence made him sad. Why did people he felt safe with have to leave him he asked? He felt hurt and abandoned, stabbed emotionally. Then he talked about his own birth mother, who was believed to have been captured and killed by, in his own words, 'men as large as giants' in the jungle of the Belgian Congo. She had been a young mother, abandoned by their father who deserted them to travel overland to reach the UK by any means possible, in search of a safe future and a better life for the family.

He told me, in detail, how the family had survived in the jungle. The last sighting of his mother — reading between the lines, was her decapitated head lying between the twins in the pram. As we spoke we found the two of us had much in common, the difference in our skin colour made not an iota of difference. The room fell silent; I felt in some way a deep sense of responsibility for my three companions in the room.

I discovered that a boarder could move from one dormitory or bedroom to another provided the request was made formally to Captain Frost; rarely was it turned down, unless age was a concern, or race. The latter was forbidden if a room had all whites or all blacks as this perhaps trigger gang warfare, or at least separate the boys by colour. The matter was usually dealt with by common sense. A few boys had moved in after Johnny left I was now the eldest by age and an expected long-termer, owing to my interest in studying to become a primary school teacher, the final decision according to the Captain was mine and mine alone. Marvin, a part-timer, asked my permission to move in. I repeated to him that under no circumstances would I listen to, or pander to his fantasies about him one day owning a castle, being a pop star, or anything else his mind conjured up. Simon and the twins were at an age where they could be influenced by such nonsense.

There were requests from other boys but Marvin was the most suitable candidate to replace Johnny, especially given that he vacated the home from Friday morning until Sunday evening. Seven days a week in his company, with his erratic behaviour and tall stories would be too much for even me. So with the Captain supporting my decision, I felt good. I missed Johnny so much, but I couldn't begrudge him his reason for leaving. After all, my happiness wasn't his responsibility.

Understanding and living in such close confinement taught me that bedtime can have positive effects; lending a sense of calm and security.

I had concluded that Polo had no recollection of seeing his mother's severed head. Not forgetting, of course, Simon the twelve-year-old bed wetter. What demons had hold of him? I understood little, for he and I had never ventured into his conscious or subconscious. It was his choice entirely to divulge any of his deeper secrets to me. What I did understand from this character is that, like most of the boys at the Home, we all had a common denominator that, like flotsam and jetsam, we were all pushed from one situation to another.

From my viewpoint I was a lucky young man, both physically and mentally. I had the tenacity, tools and the necessary sense of survival. The mood in the room was gloomy, and whenever a fellow boarder or a friend left, the protective defense mechanism would kick in once again. The twins were melancholy and reserved and Simon was, well, just Simon.

One morning I had, for want of a better word, a brainwave. It occurred to me on the tube, on my way to work in Tooley Street. The twins loved listening and dancing to music and the only time they could let off steam was when 'The Six-Five Special' was on television. It wasn't broadcast all year round, much to the chagrin of the boys who shared the only television in the recreation room. So, on the advice of Judy at work I, being the only wage earner, bought a transistor radio. She suggested a 1965 Roberts model, as it was both battery and mains-operated.

She wanted to help choose the radio, an offer I rejected rather abruptly as I didn't want to offend her new boyfriend. Unknown to her I still carried a torch for her and the thought of her with him, a man with no substance in my view, broke my heart. The best solution I felt was to walk away and hide like a reptile beneath a stone. She tried to convince me tearfully, that things between him and her weren't special. I was her one and only love and of course that four letter word sent me running away in panic and confusion.

Eventually with Judy's help, I bought the radio and took it home, carefully hiding it out of sight of others in the dormitory, as quietly as I could I slid into the room I shared with Polo, who was sleeping soundly in bed. With Judy's and the shop assistant's help the Radio had been pre-tuned into the then-illegal Radio Caroline, but, while fumbling around in the dark, I accidentally and inopportunely upped the volume setting by at least two thirds while Eric Burden of the Animals was blaring out: 'It's my life and I do what I want to'. Both twins woke with a start, sitting upright in a state of shock. Jumping out of their beds in just pyjama bottoms and barefooted, their hips started swinging in harmony with the music coming from the radio,

The loud noise drew the boys from the two landings below to join in the frolics and fun. Strange that such a simple and cheap electronic device could bring so many disadvantaged boys such pleasure and joy and above all, help cement that special bond between us.

Adrian was determined that I was worth the extra effort needed to make me a primary school teacher. He insisted that a basic knowledge of English grammar, the meaning of nouns, adjectives, adverbs, coupled with my patience and diligence, was sufficient knowledge in order to acquire the necessary educational qualification. Compliments like this from Adrian gave me the self-belief, strength and confidence to continue in my quest. He also set me short tests on Maths; Geography, and English, good results surprised me for such basic understanding of the subjects.

I was still working at the factory and time was passing quickly. The weekend was my chance to act maturely, though teased mercilessly by the boys who said I was turning into a prude and acting above my station. I told them that I was no such thing and they would still get their fair quota of cigarettes from me. In my heart I understood where they were coming from. Another person distancing themselves from them only served to reinforce their self-image as damaged goods, making them fearful for their present and their future. Giving them cigarettes showed they had some emotional hold on me.

I welcomed the learning exercise with open arms. On

Adrian's advice I committed myself to exercises that looked for small advances, breaking learning down into segments. A noun is the name of something or someone and to master other elements of vocabulary would benefit me in the future. Small steps: ignore the academic who puts you down with a sadistic pseudo-intellectual realism. As Adrian said, those blessed with a good memory and intelligence who behaves intolerably to those with less knowledge or aptitude is the same as a school bully. Give them a wide berth and learn how to extricate yourself from compromising situations.

I must admit, with all the comings and goings at the home, it was hard to study in the evenings, but again as Adrian said: fifteen minutes maximum of study followed by the same amount of time away from books would rest my mind. After a short respite I could pick up where I had left off, with more enthusiasm.

PETTICOAT LANE MARKET

While learning avidly from books I still had an unquenchable thirst to get to know London and to acquire some kind of 'street-cred'. With the former in mind, it was suggested I go along with other full-time boarders to explore Petticoat Lane's Saturday market. One boy said his uncle worked on a market stall selling all types of wonderful things. So, one Saturday, around eighteen of us a motley collection of youths and toddlers, made a formidable sight, trekking across London on foot and by red London bus. Jumping on the open deck of the bus where we chattered, swore and wolf-whistled at the girls, making a public nuisance of ourselves to the other passengers and to the bus conductor, who had the impossible task of making us pay. Such excuses having been tried and tested before, were 'He's paying for me' also the offer of a ten-shilling note which put the conductor in the impossible situation of not having enough change at his disposal.

The procedure went thus-wise, the smallest gang members would ask for a child's ticket but this ruse only worked for a short period of time. Often the bus would come to a halt and the driver and the conductor, having realised what we were up to, would question us further and demand either full payment or to get off the bus ,murmuring 'Little Bastards'.. However we enjoyed the danger of getting a free-ride and chattering away loudly.

I reckoned ticket inspectors at the barriers couldn't care less about checking every ticket, an impossible task, plus the fact that I was an accomplished fare dodger.

Those from other lands often simply ignored the human traffic. They looked forlorn, probably thinking of sandy beaches, blue skies and the sense of freedom that they once loved and lost. The best way to use the out-of-date card was to mingle with a crowd, get into conversation with a girl or boy around my age; a casual remark at the right time was all that was required to appear that we were travelling together. This was a successful trick, saving me money.

Many of the older boys at the home regularly used this little subterfuge. The ticket, in its plastic sleeve had a raffle-ticket carefully placed over the expiry date. But if discovered, on closer examination by a sharp-eyed ticket inspector, you had to run like hell, out on to the main thoroughfare and jump on any London red bus regardless of its destination. The younger boys at the 'home' were advised never to use this dodge as they were too young to hold a season- ticket anyway.

Our gang regularly hung around tube stations, watching carefully for people discarding their expired season-tickets and retrieving them from a bin or on the ground. These they exchanged for a few ciggies. We were careful; no female tickets were used, as if captured the Mrs. or Miss would have been a dead giveaway.

Great fun, though given my poor sense of direction I was unsure as to where I was going. Fortunately the boys knew of my predicament and would not leave me stranded. Surprisingly the seven to ten-year-olds and upwards had a better grip of street-language and I felt ashamed, for it was they who now came to my aid; our roles were reversed. With all the hustle and bustle of Petticoat Lane my anxiety of being lost grew and a panic attack arose inside me.

The boys of my age, intent on stealing, decided that if we were obliged to split up, we would meet in a cafe at one end of the street; if need be we would hide in the public toilets nearby. The plan was to walk past a fruit and veg stall, lifting a piece of fruit from the traders' display. The women jokingly called us scoundrels, remarking if only our mothers could see our behaviour. The male stallholders voiced the opinion that we were a bunch of orphans, and would jokingly scream at us, fists shaking and announcing that the police or Fagin (from Oliver Twist's Dickensian days) would be waiting for us. I could see why we were a visual menace. Most of us were a rag-bag bunch of mixed-race kids, wearing hand-me-downs, mouths agape and facial spots. It was apparent that our behaviour and our unwritten code of conduct, with the very young small children smoking and sharing adult language, that we must be from a large community, all living under the same roof. We had all somehow adopted the swagger, an attitude of walking fast as if on a mission, that became our badge of honour.

Ten days before Christmas, it was bitterly cold and damp; the youngest were ill-prepared to cope with the plummeting temperatures, crying of the cold. One of the older boys came upon his Uncle selling television sets, the power supplied by a cable from a nearby butcher's shop, behind the street pitch, a wondrous sight to behold, a crowd standing in awe avidly watching a black-and-white silent film and Pathé News. The Uncle sent his nephew, Stevie, a wiry individual with menacing were-wolf looks, a solid bar of hair instead of individual eyebrows, with dark, menacing eyes. The plan was threefold; we were to look out for the police or any other authority that may come our way and to encourage potential customers.

Gang members helped carry the carton-boxed TV sets to the customer's transport, which might have been a bus or to the nearest tube station. The carriers were given a coin for their help and offered a greeting of Happy Xmas. The last group moved the boxes behind the seller to show activity while shouting aloud 'Last few remaining, hurry while stocks last'. The goods coming from the back of a lorry, it was fun though I felt a little dubious about the uncle's promise of guarantees. He had well-rehearsed patter, with an accomplice at hand, a man pretending to be amazed with the television's performance and another purchase was made, boxed up, ready at his feet.

We all earned a pittance from a share-out from the uncle and were told, in no uncertain terms, that there was work for next Saturday, at another location. The nephew and his band of us the boys from the second-floor landing at our home were in on the deceit. The boxes held not TV sets, but bricks, packaged in sand to create the illusion of the weight of a new television set.

How many hard-working people in 1965 were duped that special Christmas day; undoing their treasure for all to enjoy, bringing in neighbours to help with the celebration, the first television in a working class street only to find they had been cheated and their savings stolen. There was also the embarrassment and arguments as well as the disappointments. Lining his own pockets was the uncle's way of poisoning the lives of his fellow men.

I went to work on Monday morning full of wild exaggerations from fellow workers as to how our group had seen and our behavior at the street market over the weekend.

I was overwhelmed with the number of invitations from work colleagues to join in with their seasonal festivities. They also said I should bring some friends from the home. Judy in particular offered the hand of friendship but of course I declined. Having to sit opposite her father all night, wearing silly paper hats was too much even for me to bear.

When more work colleagues learned that I shared my life with several young, abandoned, boys of all creeds I was inundated with invites from all races. I invented a lie to extricate myself from the situation. If I accepted one invitation, how could I deny another so I put them off by saying I was obliged by law to stay at the home.

On Christmas Eve I phoned mum and dad in Hastings then ended the conversation with the excuse of running out of change. Marco, Polo, Simon, and around fifteen other boarders, were in the kitchen where Betty had prepared fish and chips, our favourite dish. There were no decorations at all, other than the obligatory crucifix above the serving hatch. Adrian was in charge of the celebrations that evening, with me as deputy. None of us were allowed out of the building, in case we fell in with well-wishers in the area of Peckham Rye Lane, offering us alcohol. The old captain was aware of my recent acquisition, the only radio in the house and allowed us to listen to it as long as the volume was low, until eleven o'clock in the evening; such was the kind spirit of our benefactor.

MY WORD WAS MY BOND.

My voice now broken and I was coming out of puberty into the adult world. We created a lot of fun, the youngest dancing and jumping around causing the lathe and plaster ceiling below to creak and groan. Adrian having lived at the home the longest was accustomed to the Christmas Day festivities and knew the procedure. At six o'clock in the morning some of the youngest boys came into the shared bedroom, knocking lightly on the door. Without hesitation they burst in rushing past me hugging and shaking the twins, whispering the single word 'Radio'. I told them in a light-hearted manner that they could listen, provided the volume was kept at a sensible level. Then, having washed and inspected my face for any sign of facial hair or spots, we all rushed downstairs to meet in the kitchen area, where the tables were stacked high and tubular framed metal chairs set out in three rows of five deep faced the serving hatch for the obligatory prayer service, held by Captain Frost and his wife.

We tried to sing, though I have to admit that for many years having been under pressure from the Marshall's who were my foster parents to attend church twice, on a Sunday morning, I had been a member of the church choir, wearing a white cassock of which I was most proud. To my recollection though, no other family members attended. Our service over it was now time for breakfast.

A clap of hands by the Frosts, the moment we awaited with trepidation, it was the time for opening of presents. Adrian gave me the most charming smile, saying that this is where the real fun began. With our chairs scraping the floor we stood to attention and then moved to form an orderly queue with the smallest boys at the front and so on. Each parcel had identical wrapping paper, accompanied by a sellotaped card with the recipient's name.

We were given three presents, then on returning to our seats and another short sermon from Mrs. Frost about the three wise men from the Bible, we all let rip, tearing at our packages in a clumsy way. The youngest boys screamed with delight at their new Y-front underpants, school tie, two pairs of socks and a Bible inscribed in longhand, dated and welcoming the recipient by name.

I and the other older boys laughed nervously so as not to offend our well-wishers. Adrian remarked that he now had around eleven Bibles, that being the number of Christmases he had been there. My biggest laugh was when I saw my neatly embroidered surname on a hand-sewn label in my underpants. This was common practice as all our clothes were washed weekly in the huge industrial washing- machine kept in the laundry room.

The day passed without any problem, listening to Radio Caroline, all whistling out of tune, especially the little black boys, demonstrating their agility and rhythm to the sound of the music. With so much laughter and good cheer some of the younger boys later in the evening grew melancholic. They were highly emotional and it dawned on me they were all alone at Christmas, without any cuddles or physical contact from their mother or father that was what they clearly craved for.

Adrian and I spoke to a number of boys explaining that each of them had unique advantages; we tried as best we could to support them. At one point Marco and Polo and a few others were sobbing that they wanted their Mummy. Adrian told me that over the years it had become apparent that this particular day was the worst day, apart from individual birthdays. I hugged each child, making rather absurd compliments, for example, such nice teeth and any other thoughts that came to mind regarding their physical appearance or how their parents were the seed of life and that their surroundings was the spirit bestowed upon them. Above all they were to remain positive in adversity and that we were all one big family on life's journey.

Eventually their moods improved for a while, although I knew when alone in their beds the old demon of loneliness would rear its ugly head.

By Boxing Day everything was almost back to the usual routine except that, unless under special circumstances, we were not allowed outside. It didn't really matter anyway as it was so cold and the snow had fallen in heaps. On Adrian's advice we set to work on a handmade card from a sheet of brown paper found at the bottom of a cardboard box. Everyone drew or wrote a message of goodwill to the Frosts, which was well received and a small token of our appreciation was given to Betty, our caring cook and mentor, though she was advised never to get too close to us in a casual manner. In the past some boys had tried to take advantage of her good nature, borrowing from her or stealing from her handbag. That's why a secure bolt and padlock was now applied to the inside of the kitchen door.

To my surprise and amazement, I received a card from Johnny. There was no forwarding address but even so I was so happy and taken aback that he had remembered me.

Christmas and the New Year passed and the routine of earning a living at the factory was again upon me. I was called up to the fourth floor for a meeting with the head of the accounts and wages department who told me that because of my diligence and application I was to have a small increase in my wage packet on my sixteenth birthday in a few months' time. Also my future was secure as I had been being promoted to the Accounts Department. When I'd been involved with Judy I remarked on a few occasions that numbers interested me. Thanking the head accountant I mentioned that at some point, I would like to attend college and learn how to teach at primary school level. He remarked that it came as no surprise, though I suspect Judy must have made this known and that as it was such a large company, they might offer me a scholarship, if I was determined to proceed in that direction. It was a form of philanthropy to which the huge company had now, in the early 1960s developed.

At weekends Adrian spent time with an older group of friends, listening to pop music, jazz, reading poetry and subjects that were far beyond my comprehension. I felt left out so I would take the opportunity to walk the streets, taking a tube or bus to another unknown area of London and enjoy being on my own.

I had become frugal, putting away some of my wages, which were held in an envelope in the Captain's safe. The only way of extracting my cash was by explaining why I needed to make a withdrawal. In the past some boys in similar circumstances had withdrawn their cash and gone on the run from the authorities. So for various reasons our money, letters or addresses had to be handed over to Captain Frost enclosed in an envelope and kept under lock and key for safekeeping. At the very least it seemed wise for us boys to have this added sense of security for personal belongings

My reason for requesting money, held securely thus, was that I had fallen in love with a full-length leather double-breasted navy blue coat, the trend of the Mod; it fitted me like a glove. I could discard my well-used duffle coat and feel trendy with a new London-look style. Captain Frost agreed to my request, which still left me with substantial savings for a so-called, rainy day.

I bought the coat, with its wonderful addictive smell of real new leather. By this time I had started to go out on Friday evenings to discotheques around the Leicester Square area with some of the girls and boys from the factory, including Judy. Her former boyfriend was nowhere to be seen. We had a great time laughing, flirting and using my guile to chat up a few girls, though the music was usually so loud and deafening I almost had to resort to sign language. I restrained myself from wanting to embrace Judy. Her beady eye was on me, plus I needed her to escort me by bus to my familiar surroundings. She used her knowledge of my poor sense of direction to her advantage and we became regulars at the discotheque.

I lived in hope that my old pal Johnny would just happen to be there. My hopes were dashed; no one knew of his whereabouts. Around ten p.m., after we had said our goodbyes to our fellow revellers, Judy took my arm and gave that inviting come-to-bed look. We went into a shop doorway, both cold and shivering, our lips once again sealed together.

To my surprise, for I had only experienced French kissing a few times, learned when living in Hastings, in fact thinking back it happened first when I met a black girl on Hastings Pier when I was around fourteen-and-a-half. She was about the same age as me, so she said. Ages were important; as age of consent had been lowered to sixteen and neither of us could ignore this fact, the girl's fear of pregnancy or the boy of committing statutory rape.

Gladys was down for the day from a children's home in London with fellow boarders and staff. We met on the first part of the Pier the amusement arcade, while the staff from the care home sunbathed, looking down on the pebble beach of St Leonards. We split up from the others to go under the Pier to hide from prying eyes. I was on top of her, groping in a clumsy way while trying to put my hand inside her newly-pressed white blouse. Suddenly she immersed her swollen tongue into my unknowing wanton mouth. We were both in a state of ecstasy. She then let me slide my hand on to her breasts, which were supported by a bra made of a quite thin material, her nipples erect. Putting her hand between my legs she started to masturbate me from the outside. While she was engaged in this motion I could smell the sweetest of body odours coming from within her, I came full-load into my pants, groaning silently. After this we resumed the tongue kissing routine.

In a roundabout way I asked her how had she learned such a fine art? At the home she said in a forthright manner, by an elderly male housekeeper, a night-warden, who told her that it was their secret and if she behaved herself he would give her gifts, cigarettes and money for her to buy the latest fashion item. I pursued the matter no further as it was her business and to her quite normal, in fact important, as she explained how would she be able to go to school and gain respect from other normal pupils if she looked poorly dressed?

A THIEF IN THE HOME

My coat was a dream, stylish and warm. I never allowed other boarders to borrow any of my clothes as it could start an argument about their condition on return, if they were returned at all.

Arriving home late one Friday afternoon, after a chat and giving the captain a few pounds to put in my savings account and the usual amount for my housekeeping, he handed me a prospectus about a part-time evening course at a local college, a course which had already begun.

On the landing upon entering my shared room, I became aware of tension in the air; something was amiss. My navy blue coat, my pride and joy, was missing from its usual place on the wooden coat hanger; it was nowhere to be seen. I was annoyed and started shouting that if it was a prank; I would calm down and say no more about the matter. No one owned up to the theft; however there was always a snitch or two in the group who would take delight in grassing on his roommates. Information provided by one of the twins and supported by a large number of boys that the culprit was possibly the part-time boarder Marvin, who had pushed his way into our dormitory when Johnny left. This particular boy, I was never fond of, though I had some empathy towards him as his parents had cast him aside whilst they went about building their careers. I had no reason to disbelieve the twins, Simon, or the others who backed up their stories.

I was livid to say the least but I had to wait for an explanation until Kevin returned back to the Home. Furthermore I had arranged to meet Judy and some friends to go to the West End that evening.

That evening, in the West End, I had to wear my well-used

grey duffle coat, one with buttons and loops; it could have done with a needle and thread. Judy was visibly taken aback but said nothing, which was typical of her non-judgmental way.

When I told the story of my missing coat, my work friends made remarks such as 'If we get our hands on him...' You can easily imagine the details of revenge that came through gritted teeth and raised fists. As one put it, 'To steal a man's coat was a low act towards another. Someone suggested a whip-round among the factory workforce to replace it; I rejected the offer quite firmly, saying that I would confront the perpetrator on my own terms.

The evening wasn't spoiled or marred, as I was surprised by my friends' kindness and their act of generosity towards me. On our way home Judy and I kissed, deep kisses, her first kiss of such passion; afterwards coming up for air she looked embarrassed, we were back together again.

It would have been easy to go to the captain about the theft but that wasn't my way of doing things, it amounted to telling tales. Anyway we had our own methods of revenge; mine was an apology from him and reimbursement, with his parents having to extricate their beloved from the hole into which he had dug himself. I decided there should be no physical violence towards him but he should be 'sent to Coventry' for a time - no spoken communication with him from other boys.

There was an eerie silence when I confronted him. Adrian was by my side while the other boys looked on. He denied all knowledge of the crime but had the guilty eyes of a liar. Eventually, somehow, a clever manoeuvre by Adrian offered to take him to one side, gaining his confidence and told him he would only have a minimum punishment if he owned up to the theft. Marvin admitted the accusation, saying he was jealous of me going out with friends from the other side of society. Wearing my coat and emulating my style would he thought; help him to be accepted by his own group of friends. He admitted that he had worked hard to fit in with their lives. Also he acknowledged that he had behavioral problems and that it was cruel of his parents to remove him from the family home, even on a part-time basis.

The kangaroo court was out; he had to accept no less than 'twenty-one days of Coventry' from that moment on, a period of loneliness to make him think about his thoughtless and selfish act. As far as I was concerned that was the end of the matter. I realised that, like so many of us, we yearn for acceptance and notice that while many turn into themselves, others remain positive, on the lookout for acceptance from society

By now it was general knowledge I had acquired the nickname of 'Teach', as I was enrolled in evening classes at the nearby college, admitted at a late stage of the term. One night as I returned home through an alleyway I heard shrieks, someone crying in pain. There were voices familiar to me, laughing and shouting. To my astonishment I discovered the victim was Marvin, his outstretched legs and arms tied to railings by the use of the attackers' school-ties. The boys, whom I knew well from the lower landing, were, to put it mildly, thugs who enjoyed breaking into factories and generally making a nuisance of themselves. They carried flick knives, a deadly and dangerous weapon.

The situation was serious. They had begun by beating him on his back one of the boys wielding a broken roofing-batten. In the distance I heard the sound of the bell of an approaching police car.

'The police are coming' I yelled, and with this a catastrophe was avoided. Marvin was left tied to the railings as the boys fled in the direction of the home. As they passed me the gang's leader shouted a few expletives to the effect they had done this on my behalf, repeating a 'tooth for a tooth.'

Horrified and in a state of shock I ran to the now-sobbing Marvin to release him from his shackles. I tried to comfort him and suggested going to the A & E department of nearby Denmark Hill hospital, an offer he declined. All he could say was that his punishment was deserved considering his theft and it wasn't nearly as bad as being sent to Coventry. I returned the half-dozen or so school-ties to the offenders later when I got back to the home.

The gang-leader was sitting smugly on his bed surrounded by his other members hanging on to every dictatorial word. I confronted him, remarking that what they had done was in no way appropriate. In their irresponsible frenzy they could have killed the boy, a murder that would have changed their lives.

They laughed at me in their attempts to save face. I ignored their innuendo. I was 'up from the sticks (Hastings)' they said and that I should get back to my village and plough the fields, showing how little they knew of the place, Hastings being a seaside town with its own share of knife-wielding youths. I made light of their remarks thinking it best not to be a 'know-it-all.' I told them that Adrian and I had decided to lift the sentence of 'Coventry' on Marvin, that it was now over as he had promised to return the coat the following weekend. The incident was now in the past and my word was final. I knew that if I appeared weak these 'fallen angels', would have no respect for me. The orphanage regime was in many ways a preliminary to prison.

Marvin returned the coat, as promised, undamaged and wrapped neatly in brown paper, with a note from his mother asking for forgiveness on her son's behalf, and that it would be most charitable of me if I could try not to treat him as an outcast. I only found the note sealed in a small envelope, when I next wore the coat. Written in longhand, his mother's writing flowed unhesitatingly and without grammatical errors. Reading between the lines I understood her dilemma and could sympathise with her having to put her Asperger's son into a home during the week.

THE ANNOUNCEMENT

There were only four at most looking after us at the National Boys School: Captain Frost, his wife, the deputy manager and Betty our Irish cook. They had an appalling work load and responsibilities, having to respond, keep order and show guidance about the eighteen full-time boarders and six part-timers.

My relationship with Judy was still on a casual basis because of my schedule of evening classes at Camberwell College, one or two evenings in the week. I enjoyed the classes, though recognised I was a slow learner.

When we met we would often go to our regular shop doorway, hidden from view, for our heavy-petting session, which had now moved on to a new level. She allowed me to put my hand up her jumper feeling her breasts. Whenever I tried to lift her skirt high, she would politely resist my advances. The matter of sexual intercourse between us was not talked about; I guess that subject between us was best left alone.

One Sunday afternoon Adrian and I arranged to meet at 'Speakers Corner' in Hyde Park. I told Captain Frost about it and I was reminded that I was still in their care, also that I could endanger my liberty if I were to take part in the ever-increasing marches by the left wing and anarchist groups trying to radicalize innocent youths.

Even so I was determined to meet Adrian that Sunday afternoon. With the smoke from open fires still lingering on a cold mid-February morning, the Captain drew a detailed map of how to get there, reassuring me I would be in good hands with Adrian. Starting out across South London past Victoria station, I felt home sick for Hastings. For the first time, in a moment of melancholy, I felt an urge to be back in the familiar surroundings of my home town by the sea. This sadness soon passed as I gazed out of the window on the top deck of the London Transport bus. When travelling without my fellow boarders I always purchased a valid ticket.

Buckingham Palace Road, then up to Park Lane along to Marble Arch left down Bayswater Road, alighting just pass the seedy hotel area Sussex Garden's, where I was told women of the night stood under streetlamps in the quest of the paying gentleman, hungry for illicit or fetish peccadillo's, which many a wife back home would neither understand, nor submit themselves to. Descending the stairs the bus conductor, with a weighty ticket machine slung over his shoulder like the character of a period gun-slinger out of the 'Wild West', told me I had reached my destination. I thanked the middle-aged black man for his courtesy, even though for the life of me I could not make out much of what he had said.

Having travelled so far from my comfort zone I stood at the kerbside in awe, looking at the great expanse of the Park, feeling pleased with myself for having come such a distance without someone by my side and in a quiet moment, I felt the urge to scream out loud, 'I'm Free', a pop song by the renowned Brighton group. Those lyrics represented my life at that moment in time.

I met Adrian at two-thirty at the second bus stop on the same side as the Park. I felt all grown up, having travelled across London to the designated surroundings. I was elated, and for the first time was overcoming the demons that had caused me to lose my sense of direction. Adrian welcomed me, dressed in his usual attire and centrally-parted long hair, looking every inch the scholar he had become. As we walked to Speakers Corner he said we would shortly be in the company of Bertrand Russell no less.

'Fine how interesting' I lied. I had no idea to whom he referred, he'd never appeared on the 'Six-Five Special' TV programme as far as I was aware, nor did he play a musical instrument.

I was introduced to Bertrand Russell and we shook hands politely. The meeting at Speakers Corner consisted of a lot of Marxist academics who made many long and to my mind incomprehensible speeches. I now realised that although my hair was long and I stood proudly in my bell-bottom Wrangler jeans, sporting a pure-black mohair roll-neck jumper and the obligatory torn and worn duffle coat, I felt like an outsider or imposter. The language of this mixed group, whose ages ranged from about eighteen upwards, was so intellectually deep that when they tried to encourage me into the conversation I felt uncomfortable and out of my depth.

Adrian came to my rescue to ward off those who tried to intimidate me. Bertrand Russell with Adrian by his side behaved impeccably.

A young fellow six-foot tall with long dark hair and a kilt, was talking about anarchism in broad Glaswegian. This was Stuart Christie who, after having stepped off of his wooden crate was introduced to me; he gave me a firm welcoming handshake. His Scottish accent sent my hearing defect into turmoil, notwithstanding his patience, he did what he could to make me feel at ease, perhaps recognizing my youth and attempted a slowly-enunciated and slightly exaggerated English accent. It demonstrated the kind and accommodating side of his nature that charmed even his most bitter critics.

Four years older than myself he impressed me deeply; in

his eyes I came first to recognize a sense of truth, whatever his personal views were. I asked him if he had ever lived in the area of Glasgow known as The Gorbals. Deep in my subconscious mind at times I had been aware for many years that my birth mother had lived there. He told me that the area was well-known as one of Scotland's most notorious slums. Its inhabitants often lived in such demoralizing conditions that, according to Stuart, even the rats preferred alternative accommodation.

My quest for my birth-mother and my brother, two years my senior came to a halt. I felt it best not to intrude further into Stuart Christie's time at Speakers Corner, though I was grateful for his honesty about my inquiry. I never realized that this academic, with such a bright future, would have offered me both his time and warmth, making me feel less of an outsider in the midst of the now ever-increasing crowd. A déjà vu moment occurred and my mind went back to Dr Dylen, my London social welfare officer and with a glimmer of political insight. I felt a little more comfortable, standing on the sidelines that early February morning.

After a short while I made my excuses and left the intellectuals, activists and would-be leaders, including the 'Rivers of Blood' speaker, Enoch Powell, whom I saw at a distance. I made a move to return to the home. Adrian knew my fears and failings and without hesitation, offered to escort me but under no circumstances would this unselfish offer be taken up by me. Also he wrote, printing clear concise capital's the temporary accommodation he was sharing with others on the Bayswater road and suggested that I would be most welcome. There would be no form of payment whatsoever, also that he would not try to coerce me into any political views.

I thanked him for his kind offer but made my way 'home' instead, feeling proud of the small steps I had taken to overcome my fear of failure.

Things were going according to plan; evening classes were proceeding well and fortunately I sat at the front of the class, which meant I could hear everything the teacher said. I do not have the advantage of a photographic memory so my plan was to advance slowly, step by step and good luck to those with better memory retention. My tutor and I agreed it wouldn't take me too long, through application and hard work, to achieve my goal of being a Special Learning Difficulty needs school teacher in one of London's poorer areas. To teach the young of the day was to be my vocation, however slow in learning those kids might be, this offered me the chance to give them the power of words and to never feel ashamed or lonely in a world of blatant pseudo-intellectuals who may cross their paths in the future.

Life was on an even keel; no ups or downs. The home was an easy place in which to live and I felt a certain amount of solace between its four walls, even though the boarders were diminishing in numbers. Judy and I still saw each other on a casual basis. .

The only ones left in my dormitory were the twins, Simon and I, a self-styled easy-going leader owing to my five foot eight inches, my way with words and the fact I was eldest.

In April Captain Frost pinned a note on the communal notice board saying that he had not had a holiday for at least five or six years and this was about to change. He would be replaced over the following fortnight by a relief duty-manager and two other staff, Roy, Rupert and Keith and he asked each of us to work alongside our new hosts, a file would be kept on each boarder. To my surprise Betty had also asked for time off; I suspected because of her shy nature as was unsure of working with new people. We were all taken aback at the news but agreed they deserved a break. The Sunday evening before our guardians were due to leave we were summoned to the kitchen area to meet our new temporary assistants, three men, no female kitchen assistant for us to charm. The head of the new group Rupert introduced himself and his two colleagues Roy and Keith. Rupert was rotund, confident and gregarious obviously the spokes-person of the trio. Roy was slight in stature, pale complexion and had a strong Glaswegian accent. Lastly there was Keith the youngest; he was of a quiet demeanor age about twenty five, having a bad speech impediment, scruffy of the silent type, wearing thick lensed horn rimmed glasses.

Rupert pointed in Roy's direction, apologised for his broad Glaswegian accent telling the group of boys that if Roy was misunderstood he repeat himself if needed and that we would have to excuse his broad dialect. Then pointing to Keith saying he was a new member of our happy little band, just out of short trousers having a passion for bikes but beware do not get involved on that subject. One last thing he also loves comics, just looking at the pictures if you get my drift.

That was the end of introductions and then I noticed Rupert smirked, narrowed his eyes and gave a sneaky leering sideways glance towards Simon for some unknown reason, perhaps they knew each other, I thought.

He then went onto say that, as long as we were in his charge he would be fair-minded, but under no circumstances would he take misbehavior from anyone; we were also to take orders from his deputy Roy only and to all intents and purposes Keith has no authority on any matter whatsoever as he is on a probation period having just joined my little merry band.

This was to be the new order of things he added that the three of them regularly travelled the length and breadth of the country as relief managers and that they had seen it all before. I knew that beneath the twisted harrowing smile he meant every word. Afterwards my advice to my roommates the twins and Simon was to keep our heads down and stay out of trouble for the next two weeks.

Our new temporary guardians had their own ideas in running the Home unlike Captain Frost and his staff who always knocked on our door which meant 'lights out' at bedtime. The new deputy and his staff would just barge in telling us to put the lights out much earlier than usual. A new set of rules was announced, all very different from the old Captain's lenient ways of allowing boys to run up and down the corridors, shouting and swearing.

Soon after the new regime was in place I, as chosen spokesperson, had occasion to approach the deputy manager about some minor event and was told, in no uncertain terms, to shut my mouth or I would be place on a punishment regime for insubordination to a staff member. There was no mention of what the punishment would be!

The atmosphere at the home changed overnight, with whispers, moans and a growing sense of apprehension. The leader of the knife-gang, with whom I now got on well, told me he and the boys were unhappy with the new state of affairs and that if it came to it, he and his coterie would take matters into their own hands, indicating his latest fashion accessory, a hand ring in the form of a vicious-looking and dangerous knuckle duster. Head-banging was also suggested with a forward gesture of his head. One particular nasty form of defence was to stitch fish-hooks, the barbed-wire type, into the lapels of one's jacket or coat hidden from view, so that if a head-bang was to be attempted the assailant's fingers would be torn to shreds when grabbing at the victim's lapels, thus giving time to reach for the deadly stiletto hidden in his boot.

There had been lots of accidents with knives, owing to a malfunctioning safety-catch, where the blade did more damage to its user than the intended victim. In a typical street fight those without knives or sticks would resort to belt swinging, with the buckle doing the damage. By this stage of the sixties the police appeared to be losing the battle against rebellious youths, despite apprehending those walking the streets after ten p.m. with regular stop and search for the by now common hallucinatory drugs and offensive weapons.

I had been subjected to this humiliating procedure a few times, especially when returning from an evening class and being called the 'bastard boy', when being ordered to offer my address by the Constabulary.

The word on the lower floor landings was that the relief team was shirt-lifters that liked to put their hands down young boys' pants. Rupert the newly appointed assistant would regularly enter the bedrooms without knocking. It also came to my attention through gossip that the new cook, Roy had been seen spitting into our food. When this story spread few took breakfast at all, leaving the young hungry throughout the day.

Early one morning, about six thirty, I heard the creak of footsteps coming towards our room. The landing light was on and filtered through the bottom of our ill-fitting door. A stooped figure with a balding head, around five foot three, age around fifty or so, in stocking feet, quietly opened the door and stealthily passed my bed in the direction of Jamie, the bed wetter and stammerer. My eyesight in the dark was excellent; there stood Rupert at the edge of the bed and lifting the top blanket, his hand moving to the lower half of Jamie's body. I coughed deeply and asked what he was doing. The man replied that he was on night duty and checking that Jamie had not climbed out of the window in the night.

Then approaching my bed the warden sat beside me making me feel distinctly uncomfortable. I backed towards the wall. Rupert said, quite openly words to the effect that if I scratched his back, he would scratch mine. His words fell on deaf ears, I swore at him telling him to fuck off. In vain he whispered to me to keep the noise down. A loud noise coming from one of the bedrooms would be a cue for others to arise, to find out what was happening, no one wanted to be left out of such a curious situation. Cursing me Rupert fled from the scene; he had been caught in the act

Days passed with no redress, until Saturday morning, when only the six-strong knife gang, myself, the twins and Simon were about. It was customary to have a lie in. Then a knock on the door came, a first from our new 'Screws', a name given to them by the knife gang. One of the brothers of the gang had spent time in a Borstal, told him this was what the prison warders were called when he was there.

Rupert and Roy marched into our bedroom, and in a calm authoritative manner, instructed Simon to follow them. Climbing from his bed in his pyjamas, with no sign of urine stains, Simon was led downstairs to the bathroom landing. We were told, in no uncertain terms, not to follow; this was a private matter and if we disobeyed we would be put on cleaning duties, for eight hours a day, Saturday and Sunday inclusive. Simon in his usual manner, head bowed, was led downstairs to the bathroom between the warders.

I motioned to the twins not to stir and stay in their beds. After a few minutes or so I leapt out of bed, dressed in a hurry, wearing socks so as not to make any sound and crept downstairs, each foot avoiding the creak of the floorboards.

Outside the bathroom I heard feint, unfamiliar sounds. Luckily for me the door was slightly ajar. Before me I saw the rear view of Rupert, his trousers around his ankles standing on tip toes, his hands gripping Simon's shoulders, making thrusting movements on his backside. Simon's back, still arched kept in position bent over the sink, while Roy held his hands in restraint. A few seconds later Rupert moved away, wiping his penis on a few sheets of toilet paper, flushing them down the toilet pan. He moved to one side to allow Roy to fondle Jamie's penis, in a form of masturbation, Simon made a loud moan then sighed, and was released. 'That's a good boy, you are now one of us, you enjoyed that I know you did Simple Simon. Remember you are among friends and should thank me as you are now in a privileged situation, a member of a private club, a secret society whose members care for each other.'

Hearing this a tear of hopelessness and sadness fell from my cheek, I could watch no more, with the stealth of a cat I returned to my room.

Marco and Polo were sitting up, inquiring in unison what had I found out. They wanted the gossip, be it true or untrue. With an overwhelming urge to vomit I kept my own counsel and made up a lie. To avoid further ado I suggested we listen to our favourite hit songs on the transistor. It seemed ages; it probably wasn't before Simon appeared at the door, his pyjama bottoms showing signs of bloodstains. Walking in obvious discomfort he climbed into bed, covering himself with the regulation one sheet and two thick blankets, sobbing silently to himself.

Making sure the coast was clear I urged the twins to take separate baths; they took the hint to give him some privacy. It was just the two of us. I asked if I could sit on the edge of his bed. I suggested that perhaps, having constipation he had forced himself to open his bowels to the point where he had bled. This statement was a ruse on my part.

'If you like I could go down to the chemist and buy some cream with healing powers'. I didn't let on to Simon that I knew the truth, that he had been subjected to a tortuous ordeal. I asked him no personal questions, but coasted around the subject nervously, in a guarded way.

I hurried to the local chemist and bought some antiseptic cream and moisturizer. I wanted to ask advice from the professional chemist but didn't dare discuss any details about the situation. The young blonde female assistant looked at me with open eyes; it was an unusual purchase for one so young. I paid and hurriedly made my exit, returning to the home, making sure that none of the three wardens saw the white chemist's bag I carried inside my full-length coat. Simon remained in bed the whole day; I kept the twins by my side so he could administer the antiseptic cream and the soothing moisturizer in the privacy of the room. I pretended to him that constipation was common and given time he would grow out of it.

Throughout the whole day I thought only about how to punish the three men who'd forced themselves on Simon.

Should I talk to Judy? I was meeting her that night to go to the Odeon in Marble Arch to see 'Gone with the Wind', starring Scarlet O'Hara and Clark Gable. Should I talk to her about this or wait until Sunday, when I visited Adrian at his Bayswater Road flat or speak with my social worker Dr Dylen, whose business card I kept in the safe with my growing savings.

I decided not to tell Judy of the encounter; so on Saturday night with Judy and I moving into a more platonic relationship. However she observed how distant, reserved and consumed in my own thoughts I seemed to be. She even asked if I had I found a new love. How wrong could she be?

My only craving was for revenge and justice for the harm of the self-styled mentors who had sexually violated a fourteen-year-old boy, who had lost his virginity in such a degrading and abnormal way.

I made my mind up that I had to take a stand. Although I was outnumbered physically, there would be a war. I had to trust in my strength of will and cunning, so let battle begin!

HALF-WAY POINT

The three temporary members of staff were now midway in to their allotted fortnight for the boarders. I returned just before the regulation Saturday night curfew of ten thirty, nine forty five to be precise. The stocky warden Rupert was, unusually, in the communal TV room. While not out of bounds to any member of staff it was nonetheless considered a place of sanctuary for the boys, where they could do their own thing. The few official visitors we had, or even Captain Frost himself, never used this space for his own use. But there he was, the bald one Rupert, having the audacity to sit on one of the three sofas, the torn covered one, with seats sagging to the floor, cuddling up to one of the twins, his arm across the top of the seat, in an embrace touching the boy's neck. The TV volume was unusually high, perhaps to prevent any of his conversation being overhead. Marco sat alone on the other sofa, leaving his brother in the hands of the warden.

Their backs to me; no one knew I had entered the room. I observed the situation, my mind spinning with menacing thoughts of aggression. Perhaps I should act like the knife gang members, who would not have thought twice about using their shiny sharp knives had I informed them of Simon's plight. They would have taken great delight in deploying their weapons of destruction, justifying it to themselves that it was in defence of a harmless young boy.

Full-time boarders in the care system have a special bond, whoever causes any one of us harm; we have an unspoken common denominator, revenge. Mistrust remains with us, throughout the rest of our three score years and ten, if we live that long. We were the babies from the eggs of our mother's wombs and our run-away fathers' cowardly sperm, both of whom had left us, when we needed them most.

I had to stay calm, so I pinched myself hard on the inside of my thigh, hurting myself. The pain sent a message to my brain, stopping my train of thought and giving me a moment to think through my actions. This form of self-harm leaves no marks and is better than self-mutilation. Seeing the sexual predator fumble his way around Polo's ear, as if it were act of innocent child play, a tickling game of some sort, and watching Marco observe this from a distance, unable to do anything about it made my mind up. I coughed as loudly as I could.

'Who wants to listen to the Beatles on the radio and it's live, it happens to be upstairs playing to itself without an audience.' Both twins jumped quickly from their seats and ran towards me.

'Okay let's get going gang' I remarked, leaving heavy resonance on the last word. The deceitful sexual predator of young boys was left alone in an empty room, deserted by those he hungered after. Racing upstairs we passed the street-gang members who attempted to trip us up for fun, begging for fags. They were always trying this on; it was a form of friendship toward us. Only when an eerie silence prevailed did it mean they were angry or upset, or just didn't make eye contact. That was when you had to be worried. We screamed back at them, employing our worst language. We, as well as they, knew that it was the meaning behind the swear word that makes for any hostility.

Safe in our shared room, we found Simon still in bed, covering his head in hiding pretending to be asleep.

'Zac, man, you fooled us the radio is not on' Polo said 'I was having fun with that old warden Rupert.'

Marco intervened, hitting Polo on the arm.

'Ouch, brother why did you do that? You hurt me.'

'Listen, Polo, if it wasn't for Zac you would have been in serious trouble. That man is a pervert, you know what I mean, he is not your brother man; he's a dirty white piece of shit. One of the knife-gang told me this when he came into the T.V room, and he don't lie. He's black just like you and me and just like Zac inside his heart, but not on the outside, if you get what I mean. Now say thank you to Zac for saving your black ass from some punishment. Now, brother, I mean it'.

I remarked 'Such a speech Marco, cheers fella. Everything Marco said is true, and just remember one thing, some people have a screwed-up mind, and when they come into your life just be beware; you might need to push them away or take to your heels at a moment's notice, okay.'

The sound of coughing came from under Simon's bed covers. He had obviously heard every word I had said.

'And that means you too, Simon, I've got my reasons. The way the new temporary staff has been behaving towards us especially to you, we have no choice but to take matters into our own hands. We have to hurt the fuckers especially Rupert and Roy, not Keith as he is too thick to know what he's doing.'

We made a new pact, with clumsy handshakes all round. Even Simon jumped out of bed to join in. Now we were a gang of four, our ages ranging from the twins coming on ten, Simon fourteen and me nearly sixteen, the appointed leader, one week away from my sixteenth birthday.

THE THREE ...

It was now about ten thirty p.m. and according to rules the lights should be out. Captain Frost used his discretion allowing us to chat and laugh for at least thirty minutes past the regulatory time. As we grouped, the twins put their beds together and used them as trampolines; Simon sat upright in his bed, while I relaxed, shoe-less, on my tubular steel bed.

I sensed someone was outside the door, listening. It wasn't unusual for other boys in the home to delight in listening to others conversations, a nosey act of endearment, common in most children's homes and, occasionally, a way of gleaning information. The twins were given to this activity, which they continued to do, in spite of my telling them that no good ever came of listening to other people's private conversations. Certainly, the blade-carrying gang never took kindly to this behaviour, as half their waking hours involved conversations about planning to burgle some premises or other or organizing a street-fight. They would also be talking about the girls they had had sex with, behind the bike sheds at school, commenting on which girls were as it was called 'the local bikes.'

Opening the door I was astounded to see Rupert the warden standing there sneaking about. Our shared quarters were 'Sacrosanct' as our own space; only entered by others to ensure the place was clean, orderly and that there were no issues.

'Christ what are you doing here,' I screamed. 'You're not allowed to sneak up and listen to what we are up to. Captain Frost would never do such a thing.'

I paused and was interrupted by the fat man Rupert.

'For your information I am not Captain Frost; he should

have retired long ago and let me tell you that in this present arrangement, with myself and my two colleagues to be precise may become a permanent position. Do I make myself clear?'

'Yes, but …' I interrupted.

'No ifs or buts,' he replied, 'we are in charge and you and the others will take orders from us. This place is a shambles and there isn't any sufficient form of punishment for you misfits. You see, Zac, why not join forces with me as I am a patient man who believes in rewarding those who go along with my wishes. I will show you how nice I can be.' Without any warning or signal in a swift movement, his right hand squeezed my penis. Taken by completely by surprise I shouted at him, 'you filthy bastard, you should be locked up', raising my arm to throw a punch he grabbed me by the throat and pulled my face close to his saying. 'You have a lot to offer me I know you enjoyed it, you see I can tell! Remember this what I am about to tell you, you'll be mine all mine before the week is out, got it? Good!' Turning on his heels and walking confidently away with an air of arrogance allowing me to go back into the room when one of the twins asked me.

'Zac man you all right? You see a ghost or something? What's that red mark around your neck?'

The twins must have heard but not seen the altercation; I chose in their interest not to tell them the details but explained in a roundabout way, that the three new wardens were perverts and we should be very wary of them and sort the fuckers out.

With the lights out we sat cross-legged on the floor to hatch a plan of action, with only the light of a three-quarter moon. We knew the police wouldn't believe us even if we dared to go to the local police station. Various ideas were floated, from the use of flick knives borrowed from the gang on the lower floor, or getting help from the knife gang.

By this time Simon intervened, his idea was to throw Rupert head first headfirst from the top floor of the building to the quarry paving stones below.

Gruesome ideas came fast and furious. The worst came from the twins who wanted to behead Rupert and Roy and stick their torso's on the railings outside the home.

As the twins spoke, the eldest Marco was welling up; after what seemed like hours, with the sun now rising, we had yet to come up with a plan. Our revenge had to take place this Sunday morning, as the part-timers would be back in the afternoon, our plan required absolute secrecy.

I searched desperately for a solution, but the best I could come up with was to lead the head abuser into a trap, leaving no evidence for any subsequent trial. The four of us, there and then decided to become blood brothers. A drinking glass was produced, and put into a sock, mine as my feet were the largest, then placed carefully on the floorboards and hit with a chair leg. The glass broke into smithereens inside the sock and, with the largest piece of glass; we took it in turn to offer the ritual to the gods by cutting the top of our smallest finger until the deep red blood flowed.

I was the first the others followed suit, by age of course, the last to finish was Polo. There we were clenching each other's hands, mixing our blood to complete the 'blood brothers' ritual. Simon was ecstatic about this new-found relationship; for the first time in his life he had been accepted. He started burbling about how he had to tell the world he now had two younger and one older brother, all to himself, and that no one could take that away from him.

THE FORCE WAS WITH THEM

What a fool I was, my plan went awry owing to my absurd belief that I could undo a criminal act, such as the rape of the young and vulnerable Simon. I had been convinced by the CND supporters I'd met, that violence only breeds more violence. So I tried to persuade the twins and Simon that aggression wasn't the answer and perhaps a psychological approach would be a better solution, such as sending to Coventry.

Polo jumped out of bed saying, 'Yes, I like you man but I think you are too cool, my brother's got it right see, and I reckon all you got to do is get a gun or a flick knife and get rid of the scum, especially that fat fucker who keeps coming into our room, making out that he likes us and wants to be part of our gang. He is weird and he frightens me to death Zac, or shall we run away, yes why not. Are you coming with me, Marco, you and Simon cos you're my brothers?' Simon rose to his feet and had a vacant look about him. Then Simon blurted out.

'Let's run away. Let's be stowaways and go and live on an island like Robinson Crusoe. That's it, come on we can use our pillowcases to carry food. Let's sneak down to the kitchen and break into the food cupboard. Yes, and Zac, you can write her a note saying we just borrowed the food, so it's not like stealing is it?'

This was the longest stammer-free speech Simon had ever made.

'Now my brothers' I said with a smile, 'May I tell you what I think, if you don't mind just shut your traps for once and listen'. They knew my humour only too well. Simon's confidence was growing by the minute, the twins' hip- danced as usual.

'Do you remember the problem we had with the boy Marvin, who stole my coat and was saved from a beating from the knife gang downstairs?' They nodded in agreement. 'We sent him to Coventry, walking past him just as if he was the invisible man.' The twins laughed. 'I like it Zac, the invisible man, are we really here.' Marco remarked.

Now I was on my soapbox and said 'Now let's deal with this matter sensibly, the fact is we can't run away as we have no safe place to go and by leaving we might put ourselves into worse danger. Breaking into Betty's food cabinets is still theft and if you physically harm or disable another haven't you sunk to their depraved level, any questions? If so, speak now and let's have a decision as it's getting late.

I will make a plan that might work, with minimal risk to us, especially you three. I as your chosen leader I will deal with him on my own I am the eldest and can take care of myself. The plan is this……..

Firstly the sending to Coventry plan which we have already discussed, the second plan is, we don't go down and have breakfast at the normal time. Secondly, he will then have a reason to get us up and out of bed. Thirdly, as soon as he enters the room we pounce on him: the twins will scratch his face, pull his hair, ears and bite him. This is like two girls fighting. It's true; I've seen it in the factory. Fourthly, Simon your job is to tie all the available school ties together to make a cord so you can tie his ankles together. I'll help if need be. My job will be to empty the glass fragments still in the sock down the back of his shirt. You must all say when it's over that it was my plan and I forced you into it. It's an insurance policy that will save you from being sent to a different home or worse for you Simon. You're now fourteen so you could be sent to an approved school for adolescents.

Then there is the third plan, we shove lit ciggies down the back of his nylon shirt, and you two,' I pointed to the twins 'Stub out the fags on his head, just think of when your mothers head was chopped off in the jungle. Personally, I prefer option one, especially it's only seven days until the old Captain returns. Remember whatever happens make sure none of you are ever on your own; always stick together like glue, safety in numbers and all that.

We took a vote, the twins hands shot up in the air first; Simon took a look at me then moved towards the twins. Slowly he raised his arm. I was outvoted three to one in favour of the latter, the lit cigarettes to the face and head plan.

After having slept for only a few hours tossing and turning, my head doing somersaults about what was about to happen, when suddenly there was a call outside our door; the voice was commanding. I was told in a state of urgency to get dressed as I was wanted downstairs, there was someone waiting for me.I hoped perhaps it was Johnny. All the other boys were to remain in their rooms. Apparently there was a problem with the kitchen staff and the other floors, the knife gang included, would be allowed down for breakfast in about twenty minutes. Bleary-eyed I pulled on my jeans, clean T-shirt, polo neck jumper and, as usual, put the Roberts radio over by Marco's bedside. He thanked me; I smiled and waved to my three friends, saying I'd see them soon.

I knew the old staircase well, with its carved mahogany banister; I leapt from landing down to landing, passing the room occupied by the knife gang. Opening the door I shouted good morning while they laughingly responded 'See you, teach,' their nickname for me.

The three members of staff were waiting for me as I went into the main office at the front of the building, to be met with a silent stare by our new boss; the stocky man Roy (second in command) stood beside him. Keith the cook was also there, the dribbler as we boys called him. His lower lip had a droop that made him look like a fish and he probably did dribble onto our plates of food. Here I was face-to-face with three men, whose ages ranged from twenty to fifty, I guess. Their stance told me that they meant business. The dribbler the young recruit was told in private to stand outside in the hallway on guard, as the other two had wanted to talk with me. Under no circumstances were we to be disturbed. The chief of staff Rupert spoke sharply and to the point.

'Now, Zac, my boy, I want you to sign a formal declaration in the presence of my assistant to whom you are acquainted.' On the large pedestal desk was paperwork with my name, date of birth etcetera. I asked in a casual manner, a little croaky perhaps, what the form was about.

'Listen to me, just sign where the X is and let's make this nice and easy for your sake.'

'What if I refuse, why can't I read this and bring it back to you later, after breakfast. I need something to eat first, if that's okay with you'.

His voice lowered 'No, it bloody well won't do'. He banged his fist down on the leather insert desk causing a pot of pens to fall over. 'Do as you're told now, you cretin.'

'No, this isn't fair,' I remarked, at that Roy standing behind me put me into a wrestlers hold and bent me over the desk, I was unable to move, then Rupert spoke.

'Such lovely young firm cheeks. I'm going to have my way with you here and now, and then I will call Roy; he can take his pleasure as well.'

'Okay, okay I promise I will sign, I promise you.'

'Are you sure Zac,' Rupert said. 'You have only one chance, otherwise I will give the order and my colleagues will remove your pants, and take their evil pleasure, after that I will take my belt off and spank your pink-blossomed bottom with my strap until I see its cherry red. You only have one chance, I am a reasonable man; it's your choice'.

'Yes I promise' I wailed, 'whatever you say, please let me go.'

'Jolly good, Zac, you are in remission of your punishment, or delight, as you don't know anything until you've tried it, you may come to like me.'

I signed the papers; they were release documents stating that now, on the twenty first of April 1965 to be exact, I was of age and no longer under the Care system. All my personal belongings were to be handed over to me immediately on that Sunday morning at nine twenty five a.m. precisely.

21 or 27 THAT IS THE QUESTION

My date of birth was in fact the twenty seventh of April; the three men had brought the date forward six days for their own convenience, to get me out of the way. That wasn't the end of the situation and I was in no fit state to try and defend myself. I was to do one more thing for them, they then told me, 'You have here in the safe, cash saved by you for your work in the cheese factory. You have forty one pounds, seven and sixpence. Sign the release book here'.

I signed.

'That's the way to behave my boy, and thank you for your most charitable contribution towards the National Boys Home. Yes, forty crisp one pound notes will be of service to the community.' With a nod and a wink he then put the notes inside his jacket pocket. 'And here you are my boy, seven and sixpence. Don't say we are not generous, it is for your safekeeping, after all we don't want you to be picked up for vagrancy do we?'

They all chuckled. 'Also in here is a business card of some sort. Oh yes nice Dr Dylen, your social worker, no I stand corrected, you're ex social do-gooder. Of no use to you now, so allow me to dispose of it, on your behalf'. With that he tore into bits my treasured card and other details of his address, with the emergency number for me to call him. Dr Dylen had promised to try his utmost to assist me in case of trouble.

'Now, Zac, there is one more important document for your moniker, I mean signature and allow me to offer you some words of encouragement and advice before you sign. If you refuse you will walk out of the main gate, escorted by my worthy co-worker and friend Roy, in the clothes you're standing in.' He paused, taking a deep breath, turning his head at an angle close to my face. I could smell his rotten breath.

'It reads as follows: I, Zechariah Cohen, for that's your real name. I have, for my own purposes, copied all relevant addresses of your past in my little black book, just in case you had in your tiny little mind any form of retribution. Remember too I have a wide circle of friends, some in high places, so you are now fully aware of the power I hold. I know you're a little deaf in your right ear, so did you hear me? I haven't got time for insubordination.'

'Yes I understood what you said Sir.' With an emphasis on the word Sir!

'You said Sir that puts you in my good books Zac there's a good boy, I like the sound of that. This declaration announces to all and sundry that you were happy with me and my fellow workers and that on your last day here we were of assistance to you; also that everything was in order and in a satisfactory state of affairs all round'.

I signed on the dotted line not bothering or able to read the two-page document; my only thought was getting away.

The chief ordered the cook Keith, still on guard, to tell all the boys immediately to go downstairs to the basement kitchen area. I heard the familiar sounds of chattering as the boys slipped past the other side of the door where I was being held. When the cook returned to tell the chief that all the boys were present and correct in the basement, Rupert ordered him back to his formal duties.

'Now, Zac, you kept your part of the bargain, I will keep mine. You see, I am a man of principles. Here is your bag, the hold-all that has your name tag on it, I will return it to you with pleasure, and wish you 'Bon Voyage' and may we never meet again'. The stocky man went upstairs with me to collect my clothes, telling me to hurry and to forget about folding the garments or trying to steal anyone else's. I left my radio behind as a gift to the other boys.

With one hold-all and two carrier bags Roy was ordered to escort me off the premises, we went down the long drive to the main gate. There was no conversation between us; just outside the main gate I felt a sense of freedom and elation. Suddenly he said something in his broad Scottish accent, my head spun and my bags dropped to the ground. He had right-hooked me with such a punch that I collapsed to the ground. Then I heard the gates clang shut; after that he walked away

WHO CAN I TURN TO, WHERE CAN I GO?

It was a lovely spring Sunday morning. April showers are not a myth; the next minute it was tipping down. I was walking down Denmark Hill to either Peckham Rye Road or to another Tube station nearby, a decision had to be made. I was tired and hungry, not having had any liquid sustenance or food since around six-thirty the previous evening. Had I known then what I knew now I would have eaten twice the amount.

Nine thirty on a Sunday morning is a lonely time on one's own. It was a whole five days before my sixteenth birthday and I had come to the conclusion that I was to be rendered destitute, a man of no fixed abode. All my worldly belongings were in my trusty blue hold-all bag and plastic carrier bags. I had a huge swelling to my right eye. I looked and felt a mess as I tried to hold back the tears.

Thank goodness it was a Sunday morning, one of the quieter times in London. I knew the area quite well so I headed past the Tube station and ended up sitting in the unusually constructed doorway of a haberdashery shop, it was at a right angle from the main thoroughfare, the shop door hidden from view. As luck would have it no alcoholics were around using the space. There is a God, I repeated to myself. At least I'm sheltered from the rain and hopefully, out of harm's way.

The concrete floor was cold; at least with the sheet glass window behind me I had something to lean against. Sitting on my clothes for comfort I dwelt on my new situation. I picked my nose and ate the slimy snot, it tasted salty. It was a sign of stress I suppose. I took to talking to myself in search for answers. I started biting my nails and eating the hanging skin, I really was so hungry. In a nervous way I thinking to myself that my nose-pickings would be my fluids, and my skin the solid food that would keep me alive.

A decision had to be made. I spoke to myself while looking at cotton reels, net curtains, and rolls of colourful linen, all neatly displayed in the haberdashery shop window. At least it's not a sweet shop I whispered to myself.

I was homesick, remembering a similar shop in Queens Road, Hastings. Oh! How I longed for Hastings as I sat huddled in that shop doorway, now small groups of passers-by were making their way to church. I didn't exist in their eyes, even though they clearly saw my bowed head on my first day of freedom from the Children's Welfare Society.

The year was 1965, a time of free-speech, free-love and so on, but not for me. My few belongings were by my side and, fortunately, secreted in my coat pocket was a Tube-ticket that I had picked up somewhere. Yes, I had to escape from this area; it was too close to my former situation in case anyone I knew was looking for me.

My mind was made up, no need to argue, just get on with it I said to myself. I felt dizzy; my blood sugar level had dropped, owing to a lack of food. Nevertheless I hurried to a local Tube-station not far away. My plan was to change at London Bridge, cross over to the Victoria mainline station, take the side-exit close to platform 20, walk up the busy main road to Marble Arch and cross over to Speakers Corner on the Bayswater Road and search for Adrian. Also, if I asked around, surely someone from the CND could offer me help or advice as they are a nice bunch of people and surely they would believe my story and through legal channels bring the paedophiles to justice?

I boarded the Tube without any problems and sat down clinging to my blue hold-all and carrier bags, my black eye causing me considerable discomfort. What a state I must have looked to the tabloid-reading passengers opposite. In this city of foreboding who could blame them. If I were in their shoes I would react in exactly the same way, so safeties first, make no eye contact.

As we approached Victoria Underground station, close to the main line railway station, I thought of the long walk, use my invalid ticket one more time and then to go in search of rescuers to help me. I'd then have to either walk a quarter of a mile or so, or take another tube to Hyde Park Corner, in which case the invalid ticket would have to put into use once more. After that my intuition told me I should dump it.

It was a normal, quiet Sunday morning, at around eleven a.m. Thirty minutes sooner and the system would have been busier with tourists, I had no argument with worshipers. Right this is the gateway to freedom. I said to myself, why didn't I buy a ticket for safety reasons? I couldn't have really as I had not very much money.

An eerie feeling of angst welled up inside me. As I turned the corner no young people of my age were to be seen. I couldn't resort to my usual trick of diverting attention from myself.

Just stay cool and walk through the centre of the aisle, head down and just go for it.

WHO GOES THERE?

'Stop', a voice cried, 'Just a moment son, show me your ticket now please. Thank you'.

'Here you are', I replied in my friendliest tone, trying not to raise any suspicions. However, before I could utter another syllable I was surrounded by three men, one black, two white, thrusting their British Transport Police identification badges towards me.

'This season ticket is out of date Mr. whoever-you-are, if this is indeed your real name. How is it that one so young could have paid for a six-month season-ticket? How did you pay and at which office? Please come with us. Don't say a word as it may be used in evidence against you at a further date. If the ticket is not yours you should be aware you are guilty of an act of embezzlement to The British Railways, do you understand me?'

'Yes I do,' I replied passively, I wondered whether or not to tell the truth about what had happened to me earlier and plead for sympathy. No, I decided, they would never believe me. People in my position, care-home boys, were always thought to be liars.

The officials were polite, the black man had a deep accent but, fortuitously, having been kept in the company of the twins and a few others at the home and of course my workplace, I had no problem understanding him. The other two were of higher rank, that's for sure and more outspoken and aggressive in their questioning, which seemed to go on for an eternity. My game plan was over. I admitted that the ticket wasn't mine, nor could I show evidence as to my identity, I was defenseless.

People came and went, for who knows what reasons. One female officer whispered loudly, obviously for my benefit:

'once a thief always a thief. If he were my son I would beat the living daylights out of him.'

'If I were your son,' I replied, 'Perhaps I wouldn't be in this situation anyway'.

Reprimanded by one of her colleagues, she turned away, marching out of the door in a fury. An older man of a higher rank came into the room and an awkward silence followed. Well-dressed wearing gold-rimmed spectacles, the others clearly deferred to him. Soon after another male officer entered and stood opposite me.

'So, Zechariah or Zac if you prefer, what have you been up to? We know each other don't we? In 1965, October, if my memory serves me correctly, you and your mother, Mrs. Marshall of Hastings, arrived at Victoria station where there was an altercation between you both. Is this correct?'

The room went quiet but there was a clear change of mood. They had history on their side and I was in no situation or in any place whatsoever to try and deny this. I was bang to rights. The senior officer asked me who Zechariah Cohen was; it was the first name that surfaced at the time. It was my natural mother's surname, the one on my birth certificate. A poor choice of name I felt.

'You,' the senior officer shouted his clenched fist and index finger pointing directly towards me, 'I demand answers now! Something here just doesn't add up. What have you been up to? By the way I will call you by your Christian name of Zac. Have you run away from the National Home for Boys in Camberwell? Don't forget, I have a large army of investigators at my disposal so don't try to deceive them.'

'Yes,' I replied. 'You can check with the home if you want to.'

'Thank you young man, and who is the officer responsible for you?'

'Captain Frost, his deputy, Mrs. Frost, and Betty the kitchen Cook.' I stuttered.

'My word Captain Frost,' he remarked. 'What a coincidence, I know him, a fine fellow indeed. You see, I support the National Boys Home and its operations, have done so for years. Right, no more to be said until I get back, Meanwhile get this young man some refreshment, I'm sure I can sort this mess out in no time at all'.

The atmosphere was now calmer, the tone towards me considerably more civil and I was soon presented with tea, a bacon sandwich and a bar of chocolate. I was famished, not having eaten since the previous evening. Before devouring the whole bar of chocolate I offered a piece to the woman officer who had behaved so aggressively towards me earlier. This was normal practice among the full-time boarders at the home, my offer, which she refused politely, clearly disconcerted her.

The senior officer finally returned, telling the other officers present to remain quiet, he said he would conduct the interview himself. Standing before me, his hands behind his back he said:

'Now, I wish to inform all of you of my telephone conversation with this boy's recent home, and to let you know that records show that he is in fact known both as Zechariah Marshall and Zechariah Cohen. He has not tried to deceive us; records state that a Mr. and Mrs. Marshall in Hastings cared for the boy for the last twelve years or so, and the school authorities felt it quite right and proper for him to use Marshall as his surname. Mr. and Mrs. Marshall have a birth-son called David, two years older than Zechariah and it made good sense for Zechariah also to use that name, as both attended the same school. He was not adopted and his birth-mother Miss Cohen, now Miss French, or Miss Cohen-French, was undecided as to which name she should use. She and her son have one thing in common, different legal names, which they could use at any time.

Miss Cohen French was, at that time, living in an area of Glasgow and according to Strathclyde Police, she was a regular visitor at the station and refused to allow 'Zac' an abbreviation of the longer version. The woman officer interjected. 'Excuse me, sir, but what name shall I put down for our report. I am a little confused Guv.'

'This young man was put into the safekeeping of the National Boys Home in the name of Zechariah Cohen, born April 27, 1949, so as far as the records are concerned, all verbal or written correspondence, regarding this matter should refer to Zechariah Cohen.'

'Sir' a younger officer in his mid-twenties said, 'Guv, just one question. Today's date is April 21, not the 27th as per your information sir, so in legal terms with respect, he should still be in the care system, shouldn't he sir?'

'A good point officer well observed and I would comment as follows: As we all know, many boys and girls, from deprived backgrounds, become runaways. Most of them end up here as their first port of call, they are easy to spot,' he paused for a moment. 'I suspect the boy here came to our attention as his youth is so obvious, also the fact he was laden with cheap baggage and had a black eye. He was by no means a typical young boy with a mum; dad, brothers or sisters at home in the suburbs...

Captain Frost, who is presently on holiday, is a personal friend of mine; he has meanwhile installed temporary staff of the upmost integrity, where the care of these boys is held, in his own words, to be of paramount importance.

The man in temporary charge, of whom I have no personal knowledge, explained to me on the phone that on the release form it looked like the figure was twenty one, not twenty seven, a simple mistake over a written number. Also that Zac had made it clear that he would like to move into the outside world as soon as possible, especially as he had the means to fend for himself, with his secure job at the cheese factory.

I had another conversation about five minutes ago, with the head of the temporary staff installed by Captain Frost in his absence. He was still in a state of shock, relating how, with the help of his other two members of the team intervened to stop the altercation going on in one of the dormitories upstairs that he never ever bore witness to such foul language and violence as he recently witnessed from the boy, Zechariah.

Apparently there was a fight for leadership or over a girl, when Zac fell out of favour with a gang of boys, who as gossip had it, carried knives. All this happened just before breakfast, hence no sustenance taken and suspect they robbed him leaving Zac with only the coins in his pockets.

He suggests that, downstairs in the office, Zac demanded, of all three members of the temporary staff that he wanted to leave at once, as was his legal right, being most ashamed of his behaviour and the trouble he had caused them as they were previously on good terms. Then, to their astonishment, Zac most charitably donating the sum of forty pounds, his savings, to the National Home for Boys, to help other boys in similar circumstances, this was an unusual act of charity and although he tried to talk Zac out of his decision, all parted on good terms.'

A mutter of approval spread through the room at this 'intelligence'.

'Yes I agree with your sentiments entirely, my feelings also. Jolly good show Zac, so charitable. By the way, Zac took the remaining one pound seven and sixpence for himself, saying he had twelve pounds tucked away in his jacket pocket and that he would be getting his pay on Friday afternoon. He also insisted he had a steady girlfriend and, with her family's permission, was to reside with them, and start to save for their wedding, when they both had come of age. The temporary chief of staff said he felt it wasn't his duty to pry into such matters, especially as his was only a temporary work placement, at the home. The other temporary staff have also been officially endorsed and certificated by the authorities, something that can be verified if necessary. To sum up, I think, that although we have in front of us a young man, who has indeed been involved in criminal act, but my view is he should be given a chance to pay, here and now, the fare he was negligent in paying and released'.

The room fell silent. 'As he is by law, under age by six days and they have admitted they got his date of birth wrong, an easy mistake to have made, the staff at the home have made it clear they would welcome him back. Otherwise he'll have to go into a hostel for the homeless. Alternatively we could give him a free travel warrant and get him back to Hastings, accompanied by an officer, if need be. One of my men who met Mrs. Marshall previously has just given me a note saying that he contacted her a few minutes ago and it appears that she and her husband and Zac's brother David would welcome him back with open arms.

Mrs. Marshall fully understands Zac's sense of adventure

and even although he'll soon be past the age of sixteen she will apply, formally, to be his foster carer until his eighteenth birthday.

So, Zechariah I mean Zac,' I smiled back at him, 'With the help of my staff, I'd urge you to return to Hastings, put this matter behind you and get on with building your life.'

Silence ensued I felt uncomfortable, but common sense prevailed. 'Back to Hastings please.'

As one kindly officer said, shaking my hand and wishing me luck and good fortune, 'A painful way of growing up.'

HASTINGS RETURN

My old bedroom at home in Hastings was still the same as I had left it, furnished with basic requirements, dark-stained wardrobe and chest of drawers to match, single bedside cupboard and my old trusty single bed with a hideous pink button-back headboard. No change there, I thought. No posters on the wall, as they were forbidden, no identity, indeed it may just as well have been a cell of some sort. At least my room had a view to the back garden. A huge solitary old apple tree, some of its limbs hacked off by dad. The lichens disturbed all because he felt that the thing his words were, that it was too big and out-of-control. Those terms of aggression were probably his true feelings towards me.

Things were more or less back to normal; mum was in good spirits and coming off prescription drugs, Valium or Librium but now on alcohol. She had secured a part-time job working from home with an up-and-coming student organisation, youngsters from Scandinavia, girls and boys ages ranging from fourteen to twenty, sent over to England in the summer holidays to learn English as their second language. The period of the mid-nineteen-sixties having risen with the music and lyrics of The Beatles, Rolling Stones and Bob Dylan, to name just a few, where times were changing fast, the youth of the day voiced out loud, their opinions, likes and dislikes, in defiance of their elders.

The English language was the key to employment, being based in Hastings on the South East Coast, was an advantage, as was a proximity to Dover the gateway to Europe. My parents, having other teenagers passing through their doors, should have become enlightened and have a broader outlook, alas not so lucky for me as my curfew was nine thirty p.m.

midweek, extended to ten o'clock Friday and Saturday, held in place by a severe warning especially from my mother. None of my friends were allowed to visit and I was reminded not to treat the house like a hotel. I was told this several times and she also reminded me that they could have had the choice from any number of orphans; I made no comment as usual and began to look above her eyebrows, my way of showing no emotion.

I eventually had a 'heart to heart' about my future with my mother one afternoon, just after she had finished listening to Mario Lanza. Timing with her was important, when she was relaxed and in high spirits I opened the subject of going to the college in St Leonards, only a short distance from my home, in pursuit of further education to attain my dream of becoming a primary school teacher. 'No Zac! Such nonsense' she answered vehemently. 'You have no qualifications and let's both be honest, you are a nice boy but a simple boy. I don't mean to be unkind; it's not your fault but how would you feed and clothe yourself? I told you the night when you chose to re-enter our lives from the London children's home that I took pity on you and we agreed that you were never to be a burden on us financially. It is good that we have had this little chat; to be honest I think you should be thinking about finding a job of some sort. Maybe washing dishes in a restaurant or café, when you were younger in the summer holidays you told me that you enjoyed that type of work.' 'Yes mum you are right' I replied. That was the end of any hope of becoming a Primary school teacher, instead I found work on Hastings Pier for the summer season, this resigned acceptance happened after first taking a stroll on the beach to collect my thoughts and then ascending up the steps on to the pier.

RICKY'S BUCKET OF CASH AT MY FEET

At the piers entrance a handwritten sign. 'Temporary Bingo Caller Required For The Summer Holidays, Suit Young Person, No Previous Experience Necessary, Apply To Ricky At The Office Next To The Shooting Gallery'. I met a short man, around forty to forty five years of age; I guessed he was of Irish origin, slight in frame, hooked nose and kindly eyes. I told him a little about myself. He was uninterested, what he wanted was that if he gave me the job I wouldn't let him down. I got the job to start with immediate effect, the next day he would show me the ropes and, as he said, to get 'bums on seats' represents cash in the wallet. That is the barometer of how good you are. Work conditions permitted casual attire, jeans were not a problem, tie not applicable, of clean appearance plus an ability to offer the paying audience humour, integrity and honesty. The members pay cash only, which you collect using an open bowl. Then its contents are emptied into a container, Rick's bucket at your feet, on the podium out of eyesight.

'Let me remind you Zac, I am an ex-merchant seaman and have a black belt in judo, let's say honesty is the best policy, but where it favours both of us then overtime rates will be one and a half times the hourly pay. I will pay some of this to you cash-in-hand; at the end of the season a cash bonus will come your way as well. Bums on seats! That's my motto, okay'. He smiled and gave me a boyish grin, we were I felt of the same two minds.

The schedule for work was six days per week ten a.m. start till end of business, often around nine thirty p.m. One hour break during a quiet time. About a third of my wages were handed to my parents, towards the housekeeping, more than fair I thought, especially as my main meal would be my responsibility. Mum was pleased with that arrangement. What a fun job it was, coaxing a few men but mostly ladies to take part in playing Bingo. There I was the centre of attention, with older women of all shapes, sizes and characters. The morning's first game at around ten-fifteen, comprised maybe just three or four people wanting to play. Some even had their own favourite seats, lucky seats they surmised, which I had to announce or write on a card were reserved. This was the moment my sales patter had to take shape, as an empty semicircle of vacant chairs would be discouraging. The first win of the day, in the game of bingo, was two cigarettes; I had to inform the players of prizes, at the start of each game. Other prizes were as follows, a tin of beans, vegetable soup, packet of biscuits and a large tin of chocolates, maybe a cuddly toy. Whatever else I guess Ricky could buy 'on the cheap', in a London warehouse, market or some bankrupt stock. I think for legal reasons cash prizes were on another level.

Good fun was had by all; I was liked for my crystal-clear accent which lessened any confusion over the Bingo-ball numbers being called out. At eleven thirty, tea and biscuits all round, a short hospitality break to encourage new customers, who paid well for such hospitality. Every evening at eight fifteen the keen players would come across to us from the large hall at the Pier's entrance and play like fury, as if their very lives depended on it.

One rather elderly lady, using a tubular metal-frame walking-aid would often sit directly opposite me, her legs wide-apart, sporting yellow-stained bloomers. When she left, after her typical fifteen minutes stint, without fail a puddle of urine would have dripped onto the floor. I had a bucket of disinfectant and a mop at the ready, Rick had warned me about this. Regulars and holidaymakers a-plenty, giggling girls wearing 'kiss-me-quick' hats and the older men, possibly the oldest swingers in town, the so-called Casanova's on the pick-up, what a shame when their toupees slid to one side of their shining scalps. Ricky was a good boss and a close friendship soon formed, though I never took him for granted or tried to outwit the man as I held a warm respect towards him, and his only failing, in his words, was that he had an eye for ladies with a peach-shaped bottom. We both agreed that we were of the same mind, both leg-loving men. Ladies wearing short skirts, suspender belts and stockings the seam-line going from the heel to the stocking top, exhibited the sexiest form of fashion for men to feast their eyes on, to say the least.

Life had turned for the better, home life much calmer, I became a paying lodger, mum and dad showed great interest in their new-found work with foreign students. I had money in the bank and purchased new clothes. The work of ten to twelve hours each day, with no days off, soon took its toll. I became restless, in search of something else to do. Realising by working indoors I had missed the sun's rays I carried on throughout the summer, and Rick true to his word handed me a nice bonus in October as promised all in crisp notes and above all the hand of friendship. He asked me to stay on, on a part-time basis throughout the winter months and work alongside one of his daughters from his first marriage. She was about four years older than me, a taskmaster; a little too strict for my liking and also did not care for the idea of the cash in hand part of the business her father had created. So I declined his offer of employment suggesting that I should make a start and seek permanent employment.

A JOB FOR LIFE

I was on the jobs market again, seeking work, my third time since leaving school, work was plentiful in the nineteen sixties. The older employees had misgivings about the younger generation, whom they viewed to be disloyal and demanding, with modern views on how one should work. Stop the so-called nine to five routine; marry at a young age then children. That's how I viewed it, of course influenced by the popular culture, 'I'm free', by the band 'The Who'. The young were taking 'purple- hearts', growing long hair and swearing out loud in the street. That was my world, but of course I had to try and adapt and become one of the former types.

I soon found a job at the local glassworks, in the centre of town. The job was advertised as learning to install windows; 'applicants must have good numerical skills - would suit an apprentice.' My interview went well, owing to my numerical skills, I liked numbers and was quick at basic addition and subtraction, also fractions. So I was ideal and a local lad that was the way they put it, with the right address on the West hill of Hastings, certainly not from any local council estate which was frowned upon. Start work at eight thirty a.m. and finish at five thirty p.m. One hour break at lunchtime, two fifteen minute breaks, one in the morning and one in the afternoon. The work was in the office for accounts in the mornings and afternoons, learning how to cut glass, restore period stained-glass windows, load and unload vans.

The numbers game really suited me; I was fast and for the most part accurate. I had to take the customer's measurements and cost the work, after my calculation the secretary would check my work as we wanted to avoid incorrect charging which would damage the firm's good reputation. The pay was a great deal less than I had earned at the bingo; early-morning start was not to my liking. Nevertheless the good thing about the job was a female employee, the personal assistant to the Boss. I guessed she was in her mid-thirties, wearing a split skirt revealing the seam from her ankle rising to her thighs, showing that she was wearing stockings and a suspender belt for comfort and attention and not moved in the direction of wearing tights. She had a sultry sexual attitude that stole my attention. I think she knew it and made the most of it is, as on more than one occasion she caught my eye and gave me a sideways glance and scolded me, her finger wagging at me saying you are a naughty boy get on with your work.

At that time I had a quite a few girlfriends who I would meet at the 'Pam-Dor', a popular upstairs coffee bar in Queens Road, on a Saturday night I would also frequent 'The Witch Doctor,' a discotheque based at the Marina in St Leonards, still a virgin, my endeavour to have sex with girls had increased. The 'Pam-Dor' coffee bar was the in-place to go, offering hamburgers, 'Rock-Ola' jukeboxes blaring, playing our choice of music, also a separate room to play on the pinball machines, and the one-armed-bandits, technically set to take all our cash. 'Purple Hearts' had now become known as 'Happy Pills,' an indulgence chosen by some individuals at their peril. Ultimately one such young local warm-hearted girl, aged eighteen, died from an overdose. Also on the subject of an early death hitch-hiking was a common form of free transport, this had hidden dangers when a pair of eighteen to nineteen year old lads left to travel to another country for a two-week summer break of adventure, one returned alive the other in a coffin. In Spain just before darkness fell, a lorry driver misread the road and killed outright one of the lads. I know from experience you have to stick out your arm showing your raised thumb and then moving out onto the road, this act of bravado takes no prisoners. The longer you have been waiting the more frantic the show of arm, and to some drivers this could be a negative as your pleading showed some form of emergency, for the most part drivers would rather speed away.

Some roads are just too narrow for any sensible driver to come to a halt. It was an incredible act of daring to hitch hike, especially for young single girls, a practice not to be admired but to be admonished. The worst trick of all, carried out by two or three hitchers together, only one of them, the smallest, would stand thumbing a lift, whilst the others would hide behind a hedge. When the driver stopped he would be alarmed at the appearance of the others, hence the wisest drove off at full speed.

A PARISIAN LADY

On a casual basis, working behind the counter serving food in the Queens Road coffee bar, was a woman of French origin, called Marie de Paris, she had somehow found her way to Hastings. No one knew her very well, though she had been in the town for a few years. She was around her mid-thirties, smart in appearance and kept her own council. We all knew that she was involved with a local man who was in the Royal Navy. Rumours had it that he was a tough person if you crossed him. Even when he was on leave only a few had ever seen them together, occasionally arms linked. No one knew anything about her past or where she had worked, only that she came from Paris, where she had met her sailor.

I made a decision one Saturday afternoon to catch a bus from Hastings town centre to Bohemia Road, an area of antique and second-hand bookshops, in search of any book of interest. I felt at home among the dusty book shelves and always got a warm welcome from these types of people, who willingly shared their knowledge with me and for their Bohemian ways, I felt comfortable in their presence.

Standing next to me at the bus stop was Marie. I started a conversation, I explained my plans and she said she also had an interest in second-hand books; they were cheap for the enquiring mind, also there was a vast selection on offer. We decided to go together as we were going in the same direction, then music was discussed and she revealed how she preferred Dylan to Donovan. I agreed we shared the same tastes and also I thought it was nice to hear her accent and found her dialect was inviting in a seductive way.

I never realised she could talk so much, not in an earnest giggly way that most young girls do. I was no stranger to her, referring to me as Zac. Marie asked me if I wished to accompany her a little further, beyond the Bohemia road village, going on to the area of Silverhill. Since we had a common interest in music and books we could share a few hours together at her place, where she would prepare some French Cuisine, she thought I would enjoy that. We both laughed as I remarked No frog's-legs for me! I noticed a few passengers looking at us out of curiosity. Eventually we alighted from the bus at an area I knew well. On entering into a cul-de-sac, made up of Victorian redbrick houses, that were standing proud four or five storeys high, we entered the building where she lived. She led me into the hall; I noticed the shining parquet floor and ceiling with its original white-painted coving, a truly majestic building, now divided into apartments. On the hall table she collected her mail, she took my hand and remarked, 'You don't mind do you Zac', I replied 'No not at all it is fine by me' also adding 'You keep yourself looking nice Marie.' She answered, 'That's nice to hear, it's been a long time since a boy as handsome as you has given me such a welcome compliment.'

Silence prevailed, nothing more was said, she invited me into the single-bedsit, it was in need of a lick of paint and some attention to a few sheets of wallpaper, falling away from the wall, but it was generally clean tidy and homely. Marie sat on the single bed, 'Sit here beside me, we can talk can't we, you're not frightened of me, are you? 'I took a chance to say, 'No, not at all, can I tell you something, you really have got lovely legs, whoops sorry', I blushed.

She interrupted me by placing her index finger to my lips. 'Don't be self-conscious Zac; I'm very happy you like them, would you like to see more of me. Of course I will show you.'

Then without hesitation said 'I want to pose for you.' Standing in front of me, her legs apart slowly lifting her skirt up to reveal the tops of her nylon flesh-toned stockings, also her pink suspender belt, lacy pink knickers and a pair of white high heels. It became very quiet until she broke the silence, 'There, come on Zac you've got to do as you're told,' her smile put me at ease, our eyes meeting each other's, she puckered her lips after each syllable. Then she demanded of me in a soft tone 'Lie down, and no kissing me there's a good boy' I did as I was told, now on my back, my head resting on the single pillow. She knelt down and whispered in my ear, "Put your hands behind your back and don't say a word.' I nodded in agreement and then looking into my eyes, she mouthed slowly to me, 'I'm going to unbuckle your belt and take your trousers down and see what you have for me'. This she did in a very slow way, revealing my Y fronts, my trousers were round my ankles so I was in a fixed position. She said 'I see a very nice present you have for me.'

She paused, 'Now I will give you a present in return'. She first removed her blouse and then her skirt offering them to the floor after kicking her stiletto heels off, turned away slowly stepping out of her knickers, still modelling suspenders and stockings. Then she turned to face me and came a little closer, taking a packet of Durex from the bedside drawer, slowly removed it from the foil packet and placed it on the lips of her open pouting mouth rolling the lubricated sheath onto my rigid member, then unrolling the rest by hand.

Afterwards conversation arose, she asked me if this was my first experience, I admitted the truth, that I was still a virgin, she thanked me for my unselfish attitude towards her and I thanked her for the opportunity. Marie then said that she hoped that I would strive to give others attention to detail, as I had to her, always aim to bring to the surface the needs of a female's sexual desire, remarking that some young men needed some form of guidance on the matter. She told me I was a natural, having such a nice touch. I remarked 'You have nice skin', she giggled telling me that she took great care of it as an important part of the body, not to be ignored. 'Any more questions you inquisitive boy?' 'Yes, one question, why we had not kissed.' She answered that to her kissing was even more intimate than intercourse and declined to talk further on the matter.

'I like you Zac, but we will not repeat this, at the end of the year I'm going to marry my man and please be kind to me as I am an older woman, more than twice your age, for my sake not a word to any of your friends.' I reassured her that I was bound to silence. She got up, went to the bathroom, then returned with a damp flannel and a clean towel and took my penis, wiping the end with tender loving care.

Wearing the white stilettos, her figure-hugging small pair of lacy knickers, flesh coloured stockings and suspenders, Marie took me by the hand and showed me to the door. As she stood in the doorway I reassured her of my vow of silence, pecked her on the lips, a gentle kiss of fondness and bade her good luck in the future. We were to meet at a distance later that evening at the 'Pam-Dor' our eyes met, we were formal as before but we both knew each other very well indeed and that was that. I have to admit remembering the few words spoken between us, forcing myself on any girl or woman would have submitted me to a life of damnation. I remembered the wise words of Marie de Paris, that you gain happiness in giving the other person pleasure.

THE MONKEY PLAYERS GAME

One Saturday afternoon, walking over the West hill in the direction of the town centre, I had a change of mind and found myself on the seafront, close to the Old Town, strolling along towards the Pier.

I stood and watched how a young promenade-hustler was approaching holidaymakers with his 35mm camera in one hand and passing over to any tourist, with his other hand a small monkey, which I thought was probably known as a spider monkey, imported from a land faraway. The tiny animal would grin or squeal with pain or happiness, I was uncertain, which restrained by use of a harness thrown into the arms of the 'victim.' The monkey clothed in a woollen outfit to imitate a young baby, which would appeal to females in particular.

Standing at a distance I observed the plight of the poor wretched animal used mercilessly for cash. The idea was to quickly take a picture of the scene and at some point, post the developed pictures to the tourist, who would be charged an extortionate amount of money in the process. I hated any form of animal cruelty and wanted to slink away, head bowed in disgrace at the sight of my fellow man plying his cheeky trade.

As I stood watching a trader was taking a break, leaning against some railings, he asked for a light for his cigarette, he then offered me one from his own John Player Special packet; I declined and then we were conversing. He was from the North West of England; I assumed this by his accent likewise his chums. He informed me that another member for the gang was needed, lots of money and plenty of girls, just take your choice ,I declined his offer of work even though the thought of freedom from the glassworks was enticing. He thanked me for the box of matches I had given him and went about his business.

Just a few paces away coming in his direction were three teenage girls walking arm in arm. All wearing the traditional black and white 'kiss me quick' hats, their accents were definitely from the East End of London and obviously on a day trip down to Hastings. Their lily-white skin portrayed their roots. They were duly taken unawares by the snap photographer and each took the monkey into their arms like a new-born baby, the maternal ruse trick. I did learn one thing from the razor sharp tongue of the street trader when I spoke to him again, in a boastful manner he informed me that the monkeys were injected with sedatives, to induce drowsiness, we don't want the little blighter's too lively and causing havoc.

I was perplexed by his disclosure, whether the animals really had been drugged, or not, I had no idea. Then the monkey-man had the audacity of mind to ask me again if I would like to join his group of wandering hustlers and travel to Spain for the winter, returning to Hastings for the summer. I made my exit from his company in a civil way, I'm sure he had no clue of the utter contempt I felt towards him.

PETER OR CHARLIE, WHO ARE YOU?

Deckchairs, all in a variety of coloured stripes, were lined up along the promenade in a formal fashion, facing in the direction of the sea. I grabbed an opportunity of taking a rest to gather my thoughts and to try and forget the plight of the poor monkeys.

It was customary to use a deckchair and be a non-paying customer, a prank I and my friends had pulled in the past, by running away on the approach of the deckchair attendant. When you see the chair attendant coming towards you, make an excuse and take to your heels.

With no deckchair attendant in sight I started to think about the monkeys again and the three girls wearing 'kiss me quick hats,' they reminded me of Judy, maybe she was in Hastings on a day trip. I started to wonder, perhaps she would be fooled by the smiley salesman and taken in by his charm, which would be her own affair, just let her father meet him I mused.

Without warning, standing in front of me a little to one side, a man wearing the familiar beige jacket, a shiny metal machine over his shoulder, like a gunslinger asked, not in a demanding way, if I had a ticket. I replied. 'Oh sorry I haven't got one, I was just about to leave,' he interrupted me with a smile, 'Go on, I know you don't want to pay do you or you can't afford it anyway. Have you got a cigarette? If so, we can call it quits.' 'Help yourself man, how much do I owe you?' I replied.

'Threepence, that's for the rest of the afternoon. Just give me another fag and we will say no more about it, a fair exchange and all that.' I took two cigarettes from my newly opened packet and gave them to him. 'One for later,' I remarked.

'You are generous thanks for that. If the beach inspector requests your ticket just show him this one'. He then took out a little worn ticket from the top of his pocket, whilst looking round to make sure we were unobserved. I took it and put it away. I then asked him, 'Excuse me, but can I ask you something. 'Sure what is it man.'

'I'm looking for a change of work at the moment, my job is a bit boring, you know any chance of working on the Deck chairs?'

'How old are you?' The question stunned me a little. 'I will be 18 in one months' time. Why?'

'Well they may take you on but the job ends in late September, seasonal work, there are no future prospects.' He chuckled. 'One more thing are you a student', he questioned me with his eyes, 'Or only looking for casual summer work?'

'No I am not a student but why do you ask, does this make a difference?'

He replied, 'It's just that the local council, in all their wisdom, tried last year to employ students but were let down in two ways, they only wanted to work in August, then being too stupid with girls on the beach, then not working at all. Lazy brats, that's what we called them. Anyway the office for any enquiries about any vacancies is at the end of 'Bottle Alley', just past the pier, under the promenade by the steps opposite Warrior Square. If you get there about nine Monday morning I may be able help you, if need be, the only thing is they usually only take on bums on the beat, also you are a little too young to be a freewheeling spirit like the rest of us, got to go now, bye ,'

The next morning, Monday, I arose as usual for my days' work at the Glassworks, washed, shaved, sped downstairs and took only a cup of tea for breakfast, then slyly slipped away from my mother's enquiring eye, as I was not wearing a shirt and tie, pressed dark trousers, polished shoes, my formal appearance, as required by the Glassworks, and said goodbye. She was serving breakfast to the pair of students who were staying with us. They in fact were useful as they acted as a decoy. So therefore, before she or dad could ask any questions I was gone in a hurry in casual dress.

What excuse I would tell the boss for being late I had no idea or care. On arrival at the western end of Bottle Alley, out of sight behind a wall, I waited to approach the chair attendant, whom I had met the previous day and ask if he would be kind enough to offer to help me gain employment with his employers, thus giving me I hoped a bit of a head start.

A few men arrived at about eight forty five but no sign of my possible benefactor. Maybe he was unwell or just taking a day off or late, I ruminated to myself. Then, just strolling without a care in the world, at the end of the alley out into the open came a familiar sight, yes it was, he. His blond hair centre-parted with a fringe just resting on his eyebrows, a double of Brian Jones of the Rolling Stones but of course older by a margin. He was wearing the same old torn and worn khaki jacket from the day before, open neck buff white shirt in dire need of a wash, Wrangler jeans, leather belt. The shiny metal buckle to the left side of centre was a form of fashion. The buckle on the left side of centre was for sure the sign of anti-establishment brigade of sorts. This I knew for sure as my London former National Home for Boys dweller Adrian had told me, all his friends wore the same fashion of identity even the middle age members of the CND movement.

He strode past me, I was still in hiding, I let him pass then wishing not to cause him a fright, after a short distance I approached him at his side. He was indeed a little startled to say the least. He said 'Christ man, what are you doing, where did you come from? Jesus, you gave me the shock of all shocks'.

'Crikey never heard that saying before. I was waiting at a distant so as not to bother you, it seemed you were having a leisurely walk to work and I didn't want to interrupt your private time, sorry mate.' My tongue held itself back so as not to appear overexcited or to chatty. 'Not a word about the free ticket by the way okay.' he winked. 'Anyway, what's your name?' then he paused without waiting for a reply. 'Like I told you, I may be of some help; I am pleased you bothered to come along, what have you got to lose?'

I said to him, 'You're right. By the way, my name is Zac, I really would like to be a deckchair attendant and have the job as it's only for the summer season, that would suit me fine, I can't put up with my humdrum job for the rest of my life'. He replied 'I see what you mean, I can't imagine what it's like, sounds boring to me.' We laughed, and carried on walking towards the entrance to the office. I thought I knew the area of this part of St Leonard's well, however, a concealed office and store-rooms under the promenade well out of view, what a surprise!

'On entering the building, passing down a flight of steps, we chatted a little. 'By the way, what is your name?' I asked, I paused for a response as two other male deck chair attendants were now approaching us. He spoke 'Zac follow me, the officers or supervisors, as they are called are nice fellows, casual like us, my name is Peter but not everyone calls me this, often its Charlie it doesn't matter, I don't care either way.'

'Okay, Peter, or Charlie, then I shall follow you.' He smiled back at me. The office was chaotic, but with him by my side we seemed like friends reunited. He left promptly after introducing me to his manager and throughout our conversation my spirits lifted. In two minutes I got the job, the so-called interview, if you could call it that was very short and informal. I was given a start date of the following Monday, to allow me to give a weeks' notice at my present job, they were pleased I showed loyalty to the glassworks. The only requirement was my standard issue P45, for the Income tax and National Insurance contributions. No cash in hand here as I'm in the clutches of Hastings Borough Council, discipline abounds. Good wages, forty five hours per week, plenty of overtime at good rates, they stated that I could work seven days a week for one week, into the next, no days off until the seasons end.

I would be paid the same rate as an eighteen year-old, although I was roughly just a month away from my eighteenth birthday, one of the female staff in the accounts department was a personal friend of the manager, so that was all agreed and I felt elated.

A man's wage at last, there and then, happily I assured them with my word that I would work to the seasons' end and not leave them midway in the summer. The uniform consisted of two khaki jackets, so that you would always be clean for work. On this point I observed Charlie (or whatever his name was) and other attendants, always seemed to wear the same old jacket, despite the informal request of the boss.

However, there was a great deal of happy banter in our collection of low-down bums on the beat. The last of

England's lost society of the anti-establishment Bohemians and itinerant workers. The interview over I duly left, saying Thank you, see you next Monday morning. I was overwhelmed on becoming a deckchair attendant for Hastings Borough Council.

THIS JOB IS NOT FOR LIFE.

I crossed the road, now in a hurry, passing Eversfield Place, towards the town centre; I took the route along the seafront leading to the Old Town, in the direction of The Promenade cafe, close to the West Hill lift. I was just about to walk through the alley, which led to the 100 steps taking me past the cliffs, then I would be home. An idea suddenly occurred to me, so a change of mind. The aroma of fish and chips coming from The Promenade café enticed me in. This was the café where, a few years ago, as a gang of teenagers, we would make a nuisance of ourselves, misbehaving with the two Saturday girls working for their mother, also trying to scrounge some chips.

I bought a hearty man-size breakfast and downed one cup of tea after another. I was ecstatic, in a state of high frenzy, almost on a parallel with my first sexual intercourse under the influence of Marie De Paris who was at least twice my age. My life felt good a sense of euphoria came over me, no one could deny me this, except of course one final hurdle that I would have to overcome, my mother's reaction to what I had just done. Thoughts soon entered my mind about when I should tell her of this new set of circumstances. She had recently been overheard saying that I was towing the line.

I wrote a few notes of my options on a paper napkin the written word in front of me, allowed me to see and prioritise the solutions open to me. With some consternation I wrote out on paper what strategic plan of offensive I should take.

Returning home, I felt there was an atmosphere in the air, mother sensed that, in her words, I was up to no good and that I was aiming at some form of deceit, she saw that I was wearing casual clothes so she knew I had not been to work. I had been caught out, she was not amused, hence the silent treatment towards me.

I eventually arrived home at nine fifty, ten minutes earlier than my allotted time of ten o'clock. Why she had such an old-fashioned attitude about my staying out in the evening, I never knew, suffice to say, in her defence, she was living in the past. There would be no discussing with her tonight, the two foreign students were my scapegoats, keeping her company as I hurried to be alone in my bedroom.

I duly went to work the next day, the start of the new week and rehearsed my resignation speech in a competent manner, they took it badly and tried to place guilt towards me, as they thought that I would be in their employment all my working life, until retirement. They were dismayed at my decision to become a deckchair attendant, a seasonal worker and tried to berate me, as did my other work colleagues. I was almost sent to Coventry as they felt let down by my actions as one put it, a deserter, I just carried out my duties in the manner as before.

Forty hours later I left, better than the anticipated thousands of hours over a lifetime I was expected to fulfil. However my biggest problem was mum and dad and how I would break the news to them. Having returned home at the usual time for evening dinner, my luck was in. The two girls were also present at the table and having finished our meal and just about to clear the table, I announced that I had gone for an interview, omitting that from next Monday I would be working for Hastings Borough Council as a seasonal Beach deck chair attendant. Needless to say I had dropped a proverbial bombshell. My mother held back her hysteria as the two students were present; she just slammed the door and went into the front room. My father said to me, 'Another let-down. Why can't you act and behave as a normal human being.' I just kept out of the way as much as possible after that, for the dust to settle so to speak.

LOOKING LIKE A GUN-SLINGER

Monday morning, I went through the usual silent treatment with my mother, before I was about to leave for my first day's work at the new job, she started to try delaying tactics as I ate my breakfast, fortunately, I outwitted her as I told her my start time was earlier, than the allotted time, giving me an advantage as I couldn't wait to get out of the house. Just before I left she asked me about my housekeeping. I did the right thing and stated I would give her an increase in my keep, I could see she was now becoming a secret drinker so a few extra pounds would come in handy. I stated to her that I would due to my new work schedule be taking care of myself where an evening meal was concerned, except on any day that I was lucky to get off.

I ran to work in a hurry arriving early, eager to make a start. I was then told.

'Just hang around Zac, thanks for your P45, if I hadn't received it you would have been paying emergency tax and it takes ages to get a rebate from the Income Tax authorities. Wait until those reprobates stop chatting to each other and decide to get to their workstations and do some work'. He said this pointing to his work-mates.

We were left alone and on first name terms, my superior showed me, in detail, the workings of the steel machine from which the tickets were dispensed, also how to change the printed price rolls, one colour for adults and another for children and OAPs. The machine was heavy and cumbersome, with a leather shoulder strap. The only other working implement was a two-compartment open-leather type wallet with a brown strap. Notes were to be kept in the back pocket or somewhere else on your person. All tickets sold were my responsibility and any shortfall would have to be made up by me.

My pitch, as it was termed, was the entire length of 'Bottle Alley', an enclosed area just under the promenade to the west of the pier, in the direction of Brighton. 'Bottle Alley' runs for about one hundred or so yards under the promenade, at intervals there were cast iron steps leading down to the beach. The walls of the alley were inset with glass bottle bases and fragments in the concrete. The dazzling effect was in keeping like a grotto. From one end to the other deck chairs were stacked at various intervals. The top of the promenade was also my working area, a huge amount of deck chairs had to be ready for visitors' usage; of course a lot of chairs were to be stacked away at the close of the day. The worst part of the job was when the general public took chairs to the shoreline; I had to return them back to safety, a long walk. I was the youngest member of around a twenty or so of the workforce. In their wisdom, the officials would keep me close to base in case of any unforeseen circumstances as I was so young.

I was now a fully-fledged beach deckchair attendant, wearing the brand new, work issued khaki cotton jacket, though I have to admit I did feel conspicuous on my initial outing as it was obviously brand new, but I tried to look cool and hip just like my work colleagues. I wished it had that natural worn look of the past as worn by the older guys known as down and outs, drifters and low down bums on the beat from a previous generation in the late 1950s who had the charisma and character from a bygone age that I liked. They were a tapestry of men, which included those independent individuals that drifted from one place to another.

My work colleagues were made up of several groups; some

did cut solitary figures and preferred their own company. One local fellow enjoyed the seasonal work, then went on to claim a government handout in the winter, to take a rest.

On my first day I was keen to impress, I handled hundreds of chairs, putting them out in straight formal lines. I was proud of my display and collected a reasonable amount of revenue in return. The office sent out the one and only ticket inspector who checked my progress and reported back that everything was in order. I went about my work fortuitously and would always offer a please and thank you to the, now increasing, number of holiday holidaymakers, the older male fraternity wearing stereotypical white cotton handkerchief perched atop their heads, to keep the sun's rays at bay. The day was sweltering hot, early May, and to my benefit. I was already getting a tan which I acquire rather easily, and getting well paid, what's more at the mercy of young girls flirting precariously with me. I became aware that the girls on holiday adored the machine welding, sun-kissed young deckchair attendant. My reputation swept before me, I was in my element. I had found 'The happy' in my life, I loved every minute of the working day although it was hard work at times, the best job in the whole wide world, I had to pinch myself in case it was a dream.

THE ROMANTIC ROAMERS

Through Peter or was it Charlie and his friendliness towards me, I became involved in conversation with his circle of friends, a group of older men who accepted me unknowingly. I just seem to fit in with this group of around six men; I started to become infatuated by their way of life.

I was the youngest by at least a decade or so. We used to meet at the cafe on the entrance to the Pier, the former 'Ball-Room' for our informal break; they talked about so many subjects, politics, religion and the arts. My hair grown to shoulder-length still parted to one side, wearing Wrangler jeans and a T-shirt. On hot days, a pair of jeans shortened in length to just below the knee and the obligatory leather open 'Jesus boots' or 'Desert wellies'. Yes! I could say I had found my own sense of fashion. My parents, of-course, were most dismayed at my long hair and angered by my new found sense of style. A drop out in the making they remarked!

For the first time since Adrian, Johnny and my other friends at the National Home for Boys in London became bonded as blood-brothers with a penknife; these workmates were now my closest friends. What their past was, and who they really were didn't matter to me as I felt comfortable in their presence. I held those fellows in awe but retreated from any form of infatuation. Often after work I would meet up with them and have a few drinks at the Lord Nelson public house our chosen haunt in the Old Town.

My pitch was becoming earmarked by foreign students, who heard on the grapevine of a particular youth of the day, I appeared a young dropout in the making. I would be asked if I would introduce them to my young mates. Many courtships between Hastings teenage boys and the girls from across the sea were in abundance.

I liked to spend time in 'The Pump House', 'The Anchor', or 'The Lord Nelson' pubs, and also the 'Pam-Dor' coffee bar, playing the pin-ball machine, listening to music from the Rock-Ola juke box. The local girls often frequented these haunts and were not in fear of berating me for disowning them. 'Wait till the winter Zac when that lot have gone home, 'spoken with an undercurrent of aggression. 'You wait Zac, no sex for you in a doorway on a dark winter night'. I just laughed at them which annoyed them even more. .

Naturally, the local girls, a few of whom I had dated on a casual basis in the winter months, were not enamoured with the new bevy of beauties taking over the town and their boyfriend material taken away from them.

One afternoon I asked one particular student 'Where are you from what's your name and more to the point, are you free tonight, I can show you the sights, then you can tell me all about Sweden, not the boring stuff just about music and so on.' A date was made for that evening outside the cinema in Queens's road, though I wondered if she would turn up, was she was just a tease and was she too young to behave like Marie de Paris.

It was my first date with Annika; she was wearing a see-through dress, her long blonde hair parted in the center and a curvy slim figure. She had that affable smile that says come and take me if you dare. I was at her mercy. She spoke in a feminine tone that weakens even the hardest of men and made me hunger for her even more.

'I think you are late, had you forgotten about me Zac? If you're tired we can skip the cinema if you want'.

'No', I replied. 'It's really okay; I've just had a drink with my workmates, an after-work ritual. Let's go and see the film, I'm told it's had some good reviews,'

We paid for our tickets separately. Annika said it was customary in her home country of Sweden; after all this was the 1960s, the start of the emancipation of women and the permissive society.

The usherette's torch pointed to the back row where a few couples stood up to allow us to pass to the end of the seating area. Annika sat next to the wall. The film had just started with the Pathe News cockerel screaming its head off. The lights dimmed and the film began.

'I hope, Annika, you're not frightened of the dark', I whispered. 'Can I hold your hand?' She smiled and said 'Of course'.

After thirty minutes or so we were kissing, breathing heavily, then for the rest of the film we just sat hand in hand like any other couple.

On leaving the cinema she asked if I would walk her back to her host family's home, adjacent to Alexandra Park, which I did, arriving there by about ten forty five, just inside her curfew. We arranged to meet up the following evening. I discovered later that she was nineteen years old and in a long-term relationship with her boyfriend in the north of Sweden.

I walked home towards the West Hill, past the crumbling ruins of Hastings Castle. I was just turned eighteen and fit owing to my work, so the steep hill wasn't a problem. I was reaching my prime. Unlocking the front door I stealthily made my way upstairs to my bedroom in the dark.

In the morning I was about to leave for work, wearing the standard issued khaki cotton jacket when, suddenly, my mother began berating me for wearing it, showing I was just a Hastings beach deckchair attendant. What would the neighbours say? What was I thinking? Not wanting to have a full-scale row, as it would have been a one sided argument anyway, indicated by the aggression in her voice. Walking away from me and slamming doors was her normal response, the silent treatment ensued afterwards. So, to make her feel better, I packed my jacket into an old leather rucksack and waited until I had turned the corner, by the shelter on the corner of Priory Road, well out of sight of her beady eyes, before putting it back on.

TRUCE AT HOME

After work I hurried home, arriving early for a quick wash and shave to be fresh and welcoming. I wanted to impress Annika. Maybe tonight we can move from foreplay into something more adventurous. The cunning in me saw no guilt or, as Rick from the pier bingo once stated 'A standing prick knows no conscience.'

'Hi mum', I called from the hallway.

'You're too late for dinner anyway,' she replied. 'Why didn't you call to say you wouldn't be home for tea?'

'Sorry, it was a spur of the moment decision, anyway, it's okay; I'll get something to eat at the 'Caprice' in Queens Road later on,'

'And what time did you get in last night? Don't lie to me, I know, it's not good enough, treating our house like a hotel. We're not putting up with it. I expect you're taking drugs with your so-called new found friends. Look at them, they are a mess. Anyway, they are old enough to be your father. Just what have you got in common with them? They're really dirty old men drifting from one town to another, look at the state of them, unkempt long hair; no good to man nor beast.'

Taking a deep breath she added: 'I've had my say and that's that. I don't want to hear any more excuses or lies from you'. With that she slammed the door and walked away. Her shaking hands and trembling voice told me, once again, that demons inside her mind were again rearing their ugly heads.

I looked at myself in the mirror, a vain youngster just seventeen. My slim build height 5'8" and as a result of much-needed elocution lessons, owing to a speech impediment when a child, I now had a cut-glass accent. A sun-tanned olive skin and high cheekbones gave me a slightly Mediterranean appearance, at least that's what I was told by my first learned sex fiend, Marie De Paris. This was my moment, not to be missed. Life is no rehearsal as they say. What made me uncomfortable was my lack of intellectual achievement and the fact I felt I had no natural learning abilities for anything that most take for granted. My poor memory created so many barriers, especially regarding anything technical.

That evening, before meeting Annika, I walked over the hill, down town to the 'Pam-Dor' coffee bar, I had been informed that Marie de Paris would be there, her last night at work, before moving away with her sailor, for his Naval posting abroad; at least I could look and feast my eyes on her for the last time.

At the 'Pam-Dor' coffee bar the jukebox was playing the Yard birds 'For Your Love'; the aroma of hand rolled cigarettes and pipe tobacco smoke was in the air, filling everyone's lungs. It was cool to be a Bohemian, though self-important mods and rockers were still around. After the Teddy-boy era, with its Beatniks and Mods & Rockers, it was now the time of the freedom-loving and colourful Hippies.

The last week of August was when most foreign students, visiting Hastings and St Leonards, left to return home and for me, my job would last another five weeks. By October I would be looking for another job; no problem, there was plenty of work around and moving from one employer to another seemed to be the order of the day.

'You're really looking great,' I said when I greeted Annika, taking her hand once more we were salivating over each other, our eyes revealing all.

'Where are you taking me, you naughty English boy?' she said

Laughing aloud we squeezed each other's' hands. Although I was still under the drinking age by around six months or so, this had never stopped me from going to pubs, especially in the Old Town, with Annika by my side, looking her age of nineteen. We shared a few drinks and I introduced Annika to a few of my ex-schoolmates and other fellow teenagers I knew around town. They would wink at me or blatantly say to me that my blonde, blue-eyed, long-legged adorable Swedish girl student was indeed an absolute stunner.

Annika told me that her boyfriend of two years had been called-up to the Swedish army and was based in northern Sweden, on the Finnish border. National service in Europe was common, although in England this had ended in the early 1960s. When I inquired about her faithfulness to him she replied that the saying was 'It doesn't count away from home'. Her conscience was clear, I imagined. If she got the required grades she would go to university in Uppsala, west from Stockholm, where she lived with her parents. She wanted to become a veterinary surgeon and have her own practice.

'Give me animals any day, present company excluded'. She looked directly into my eyes.

In the 1960s Sweden's youngsters were encouraged to pursue academic careers, and immigrants from war-torn countries were welcomed to help meet the shortages in the labour market. I was enchanted by the picture Annika painted of Sweden. It was a country I was anxious to see for myself.

'It's such a beautiful evening,' I said after a few drinks at the 'Lord Nelson' pub, 'Why don't we walk over to the fishing huts at Rock a Nore and have a paddle.'

With my jeans rolled to my knees and her hitching up her skirt, we entered the not too cold water, splashing each other and laughing. We found a place to hide, wedged between two boats. A few moments later we were laying on the beach hugging, our tongues probing each other, she was biting my face in a tender but brutish manner. Suddenly, she took my right hand and plunged it under her white flowery dress, into her knickers, a direct hit, her pubic hair and thighs moistened by her sexual arousal. Without hesitation I finger-bated her slowly then increasing in speed with my index finger, moaning loudly she put her hand on my wrist and in a fury we were both masturbating her. Then, with a deep sigh of relief, it was over. Holding her tightly I stared into her beautiful blue grey eyes. Later she told me it was the coldness of the water that had done the trick. Occasionally, in the shower back home, a blast of cold water would entice her into such an act.

Walking her home along Queens Road past the 'Pam-Dor,' we talked about intercourse she reiterated that this was something reserved for her boyfriend back home. We agreed to meet up for the penultimate evening before she left for Tilbury Docks and her journey home to Sweden. Annika diverted my attention, away from the usual after-work drinks with my friends, the Romantic Roamers but I felt sure that they wouldn't hold a grudge.

Our last evening together was light-hearted and jolly. We were part of the crowd rocking to the jukebox at the 'Anchor' pub spilling out onto the street, making a public nuisance of ourselves. There was never any violence as we were just enjoying ourselves.

Hastings is renowned for being laid-back; the old town is a magnet for those wishing to live the Bohemian life, perhaps that's why there is an area called Bohemia road, with its antique shops and second-hand booksellers. Nearby St Leonard's is known for its melancholy seafront and the splendour of the characterful 'Burton' area with its large formal houses, some now converted into bedsits. It was a known fact that on the platform south-side of Warrior Square Railway Station's concourse, there were no ticket barriers which attracted fare-dodging passengers, including myself. We considered it more an act of bravado than petty crime.

I tried to pinpoint why I liked Annika so much; then it came to me. Not only was she very attractive it was her intelligence that captivated me.

On our last night together she wore her most sensual dress, demurely. I was smitten by this high priestess of sexuality. As the evening progressed we tantalized each other sexually.

On our way back to her host family's home we walked hand in hand in the moonlight, into Alexandra Park, through the huge pair of red brick Piers, heading towards the boating lake. Turning left by the public toilets, going up towards Lower Park Road, we found an ideal spot behind bushes. She stood leaning against a tree where we kissed, deeply and wistfully, our hands sliding over each other.

That was the last time we were together, as she had to return to Sweden. Annika left Hastings the day after, by coach to Heathrow and from there flew on to her hometown of Lund in the south of Sweden, not far from Stockholm.

There was now only three weeks left before the summer's season ended all that remained, from October to April was a skeleton staff of a few men paid by the Hastings Council to repair the chairs. They offered me a full-time position, but I turned it down, I had a better idea .I was seventeen and a half and no amount of cajoling would entice me to settle down. Because of my love of old antiques, books, paintings, etcetera which gave me enjoyment, I did speak to my mum about opening a junk shop but on no account would she allow that while I lived under her roof.

What did she expect me to do for work? I needed to tax my brain, the money came second. Did she expect me to go back to work on the pier Bingo or worse still, claim unemployment benefit?

'No' she said 'No claiming benefits my lad and bringing shame to my doorstep', she reiterated. 'What would the neighbours think?'

SEASONS' END IN THE PIER CAFE

An easterly force-eight gale was blowing through the English Channel, our start time was nine o'clock but the workforce usually turned up between nine fifteen and nine thirty when it was a rainy day. The inspector strode up to us saying.

'Gentleman, can we have some hush please. I can't talk above the noise you are making. I suggest you go to your usual workstations until you see fit to put out the chairs we hope you'll be able to hire out today. However, if the weather carries on like this you have two options; take the day off without being paid, those who choose this option can leave now', silence, no one moved.

'The second option, if you are still in the vicinity of your designated pitch and available for work until four p.m., you will be paid as normal but you must return here no later than three forty five' He coughed. 'You see, the boss likes an early finish.' He coughed again.

We knew what he was up to. Without any rehearsal we all coughed in unison, he got the message and told us to go about our day and try not to drink the Pier cafe dry. We laughed, he was used to handling the men, most of whom were regular seasonal workers he knew well and liked. Also, the 'low-down bums' as he called us, were useful inasmuch as they were casual labour. We filled a very much needed gap in the workplace.

So it was a day to be spent on the pier, in the huge cafe seating area created from the now defunct ballroom. The rain fell in torrents as we ran along Bottle Alley, our group in khaki jackets worn out and torn at the knees jeans and of course, our leather-strapped sandals.

On arrival a kitty was organized; each of us putting into the pot the same amount and ordering and helping ourselves to tea, coffee, sandwiches, and cakes, taking what we needed, grabbing more than one's fair share was just not done. It was the same when we met up at any other pub or café where we congregated.

Two tables were quickly shunted together by the steel-framed windows, looking out towards the beached fishing boats, at the Rock 'a' Nore end of the old town. My curiosity got the better of me as we sat around the table that afternoon and I began to enquire about my new friends' past lives and how they had they become of no fixed abode. I must have struck a chord with them that day.

Every storyteller needs an appreciative audience. So what better way to fulfill one's desire, than the audience in question has nowhere to hide among friends?

One of the group stood up to speak. 'Okay Rex, you've got everyone's attention, all you're going to get, so get on with it man and please, for goodness sake, try using the Queen's English so we can understand you. Your rapid-fire Liverpudlian accent forces me to put my hands to my ears; get on with it man, or I'll take the floor myself and give you all a few lines of poetic verse.'

After a bit more banter between Rex and old George, the former leaned forward on the table, palms outstretched. 'Ok, so now I will begin'… we all yawned in unison.

'I'm very proud of my home town Liverpool. You see I am well known as a kindred spirit to the four Beatles. In fact, if I hadn't chosen my given path, who knows, they would most likely have invited me to join their band. Then, my fellow dropouts, you would not have had the good fortune of enjoying my company at this moment in time,'

Someone asked: 'What has that Scouser just said, I didn't

understand any of it.'

Rex hesitated for a moment then laughed out loud; we all joined in, indeed this was going to be a long afternoon of tomfoolery.

'Anyway, it's true that I am a Scouser and I'm proud of it. In fact, I will enlighten all of you, assuming you are of standard intellect.' He paused, waiting for a reply, which duly came from every quarter, some of the group were booing him others laughed.

It has to be said, we were a scruffy lot with the obligatory hand-rolled cigarettes, tightly held in the corners of our mouths and ash dropping all over the tables.

Rex had an audience of around thirty to forty people; apart from ourselves as the general public were taking shelter. He had a scraggy but handsome tram-lined face, with a mixed-race complexion. His curly jet-black hair and his engaging swagger befitted the culture of his once migrant family from distant shores, in far-off times.

His boasts as to being attractive towards the opposite sex was his trump card which, without hesitation, was the Ace he played at all times. He was around thirty-eight years old, and of muscular build, which his next-door bedsit mate would vouch for, hearing his keep-fit antics through the adjoining wall. Rex performed arduous press-ups. Standing now at the end of the rectangular plastic- top table, he began his performance. All eyes turned to face him.

He continued, with a cheeky grin: 'I understand you seek to acquire the knowledge of a secret, very secret language; Liverpudlian back-slang, as evolved over the years by the good and honest people of Liverpool.'

We were surprised. Is there such a thing? Was Rex

fantasizing at our expense? Our ears pricked up, he had us on the edge of our seats.

'For the sake of my compatriots I will endeavor to make myself understood, in an accent befitting my audience. As I have already said, it is a secret language on a par with the Cockney- rhyming-slang of London's East End. This is the main gist of it'.

'Get on with it Rex' said an increasingly impatient old Harry. 'Enough of your introductions just get on with it.'

'Right, this is it. Two letters only will change any word you care to choose. They are A and G in that order.'

He paused; we were all puzzled by the statement.

'What on earth do you mean Rex' shouted out George.

Rex elaborated 'AG after the first letter of a word. Fred for example is pronounced Fragged, police paggolice and so on. So what is your name young lady?' he directed the question to a young girl of around twelve years of age sitting at a table with her family close to us.

'Lisa', she replied.

'So that would be Lagisa then,' he announced, then pointing to a girl sitting next to her.

'Carol,' she said. 'So that would be Caggarol.'

The audience began to get the message and everyone applauded his presentation, the group began to disperse, with Tagged (Ted) chatting to Baggilly (Billy), and so on. I was intrigued as to how 5ft tall Rex had ended up in Hastings.

'I come from a working-class background in Liverpool,' replied Rex 'the slums, old tenement buildings which should have been pulled down for redevelopment after the war. My mother was by now a young widow, just about able to take care of me.

We were a poor family but I never went hungry as my mother a devout southern Irish Catholic was a hard-working woman who held down three jobs. She was a fiery spirited woman with hair as red and bright as burning embers on a coal fire. She gave birth to two of us, my sister and me. My sister still lives in Australia so I understand. Mind you, I'm not too sure of this as my mother had an almighty row with her after my sister fell in love with a much older married man. After having been caught out by his wife, they fled, avoiding the scandal to create a new life for themselves, without leaving a forwarding address.

You see my good looks, my black curly hair and the physique of an Adonis. 'We chuckled. 'Yes, my handsome looks, please no more laughter, let me finish.' We fell silent as he continued.

'My dad was from an island in the Pacific Ocean, Zanzibar, at least that's what my mother told me. I left school after my fourteenth birthday and found work at the docks as an apprentice welder. It was a fine job too, suspended on a wooden platform by six rope cables. An authorized welder took me through the art of welding, explaining the rods used for various types of steel. By the way, sorry I digress. My father died of a rare blood disorder, a Western diet and lack of sunlight exacerbated his illness, taking him to the depths of darkness. Sadly we had to bury him in a local cemetery close to home, not his homeland in Zanzibar. My mother eventually returned to her roots in Southern Ireland to be held in the arms of her then ailing mother and father. They passed on within months of each other, so my mother now lives in the middle of nowhere, in the County of Cork, growing herbs which she sells in the local market and tending to her smallholding, digging and stacking peat skimmed from the top of the bog, to burn in the harsh winter months. It's hard to keep in contact as there are no phone boxes in or close to her village. I try to go to Ireland whenever I can, maybe every three or four years.

I was called up for National Service at the age of eighteen, I enjoyed the discipline the army instilled into us; it was for our well-being. Cleanliness was of the utmost importance, as was training for a career. I was good at sports, particularly cross-country running with a backpack full of rocks. It helped me understand something of my own strength and staying-power. After the compulsory two years of National Service, I signed up for seven more years and I promised myself I'd save a lot of cash and keep off the hard stuff. Drinking too much whiskey would end up with me wanting to pick a fight with the biggest man in the public house, which wasn't a good plan. When drunk I was sometimes knocked out for the count. I learned my lesson, no hard liquor for me, just a glass of real ale. That was two years ago. I found I couldn't settle, so now wherever I lay my head is my home. I came to Hastings because of a good friend, Billy. We have a lot in common, both of us stand out as different; me with my mixed-race looks, and him with the tall physique and unusual features of an albino Negro.

We faced a lot of racial abuse at the time, especially at primary school. Often we would have to stand back to back to defend ourselves. Billy's muscular arms, with their long reach, could deliver a killer punch to the nose of our offenders, coupled with my lack of height, which I made up for with speed and formidable aggression; this meant we usually beat off our aggressors. We became long-term friends and well known in the locality. Billy lives here in Hastings now, working on a building site as a hod carrier. He's a bit of a lad with the ladies, who just fall into his arms, lots of great banter.

In the army I joined The Royal Engineer Corps; I'm one of those that build bridges, irrigation systems and so on. So my plan is in the near future I'll do whatever I can to help people in Africa and other deprived areas of the world. My father always told me it in his homeland, Zanzibar, you were expected to smile at strangers in the street; it was a kind of gift, something that so many people here in England seem impervious to.'

'So how do you intend going about this form of philanthropy?' interrupted Harvey. 'I may be able to help you, if you like.'

'Thanks Harvey. I have no idea what do, only that with my savings I'd hitchhike to Africa. All I need is a tent, sleeping bag, and passport and off I go.'

'There is an organization I can put you in touch with. My brother is involved with the VOS, the Voluntary Overseas Service. You don't get paid, just food, shelter, hard work, smiling faces, and even wine. A sing-song around the camp fire, for comfort perhaps and maybe even a nightcap with another female charity worker, who knows.'

'Thanks Harvey,' said Rex. 'Fantastic. I know I can do the work and I've no commitments other than to my mother. I promised I would visit her every now and then and make sure she is alright. I've been sending her postcards. Sometimes I get a reply. She knows my Church Road address in St Leonard's, where I am staying, next - door to you. My apologies for the noise I make, doing my physical exercises in the evenings but unless I do them I can't sleep. That's the legacy the army left me with. Mind you I can think of a better way to amuse myself in the twilight hours, with a fine woman, that's for sure.'

As it was getting close to four p.m., and with Rex's language drifting into the obscene and more parents and children were coming into the café, we collected our spent dishes and dirty ashtrays and returned them to a grateful café-owner at the counter.

A FOND FAREWELL

On the first Sunday in October, we were informed that we had to collect our P.45 Income Tax documents the following Monday, anytime between nine and two o'clock. That would be the end of our commitment to Hastings Borough Council. It was the last time we walked through 'Bottle Alley' after our day's work ended at four-thirty p.m. I felt sad walking through the Alley towards the Old Town with my friends. It was a unanimous decision to spend our last evening together at the 'Lord Nelson'. The landlord, an ex-police officer, was open-minded as far as dress code was concerned. We wore our khaki jackets, which we were allowed to keep; they were of no further use to the council. My friends were the most unlikely mixed group of men, some bearded others just unkempt itinerants, eccentrics, academics and the down and outs of the nineteen-sixties.

We arrived early to find the pub almost empty. Most drinkers would have made an effort to wash, shave, and throw on some aftershave to attract the opposite sex. Not us; we had no hidden agendas, no wives at home, wondering what we were up to, regarding affairs of the heart and lust. If anyone outside our group, intruded into our space wanting a free drink, then under no circumstances were any given out, as they had been paid for from our kitty. The evening's rules were set; table service the amount of cash to be spent, sorted out beforehand. There was never any trouble. Occasionally an inebriated youngster, unable to hold his drink, would try to muscle-in on our conversation but would be told politely to clear off, it was a private party. The intruder usually took the hint when they saw the size of Rex and old George. The landlord knew he could rely on us to behave well, looking at my adopted friends; only a fool would meddle with them.

The long rectangular walnut top-table was ours. It was far enough away from the noisy jukebox to allow us to listen and to sing along to the pubs entertainment, Johnny's vocals with Bruce on guitar. My favourite was 'Ghost Riders in the Sky'. Johnny, a bespectacled, well-built northerner, had a fine voice and when the hat was passed around, after their performance, most folk dug deep, but some didn't. Shame on them I remarked to myself.

I was on draught Guinness; others drank local Cider or Beer, while Harvey's tipple was Port. An old red beret filled with cash, our kitty, had pride of place on the table. Most of it would be spent during the course of the evening; any leftover would be divided up and returned to each of us at the end of the get together.

Rex stood up to say he had an important announcement to make.

'Thank you one and all,' he said in his broad accent, music to our ears. 'I propose a toast. We've not had Zac in our company for a few evenings, until yesterday. Has he been at sea? Lost? Or off in a faraway land unknown to mankind.' He chuckled. 'Or with female company in the evenings, at which I suggest he was under the spell of whom or what.' He smirked. 'Here endeth the first toast of our last evening together and, by the way, welcome back Zac, back to the fold of the Romantic Roamers of whom you are the youngest and founder member.'

With raised glasses we all chanted together 'A jolly good fellow, so he is ...'

Seriously out of tune it was the worst rendition imaginable. We were raucous and loud, but no one seemed to take offence.

Thank you, one and all.' I tried, unsuccessfully to imitate Rex's accent. 'I'm grateful to you all that in the first place you have noticed my absence from our sect, a secret society no less, but I had a love-call, or to paraphrase, lust seized me my hand, so what choice did I have. You've all been as young as me once, so you must appreciate the predicament in which I found myself.'

Old George the American stopped me in my tracks. 'I never realised you were so loquacious, Zac. If that's what lust offers throw some my way ... and for your information, young man, I'm not too old to show you a thing or two. There's life in the old dog yet.' Everyone laughed out loud.

I took advantage of this unique situation by probing beneath the surface of these men I had befriended, stories about their past and what the future might hold for them. I looked earnestly into their faces, knowing that our five-month friendship would end in a matter of hours, probably forever. This had been made clear to me repeatedly: no point of contact, no phone numbers, postcards or any letters would be forwarded. The past was the past but who knows, some stroke of fate might mean our paths would cross again. I was relishing the atmosphere as much as possible. Throughout the summer each and every one of these men had been my mentor without me realizing it.

Their stories weren't tall tales; they had too much detail and clarity, proving to me that each storyteller had been where they said, and experienced the events they talked about. I knew they kept some elements of their past to themselves, some things weren't spoken about. We all have our secrets, but each and every one of my companions had one thing in common, they were all at ease with themselves and with me.

Old George was an American citizen, a heavy drinker with goat-like features. Now in his sixties he had arrived, aged 11, in New York from Lebanon, with his mother and sister in the 1920s. He never mentioned his father, so this made him American of Arab descent. In his early youth in the 1930s he became highly proficient in backstreet, bare-knuckle boxing. He still had a muscular build. He had married young but owing to his prolific playing around with other women, the marriage ended in divorce. Without contact with anyone from his past, he sought solace at the end of a bottle. Unable to find work he left the United States for good and travelled around the Mediterranean countries, doing casual work, until finally he arrived in Athens.

One sunny afternoon while sitting on a park bench, he found himself in the company of another street drinker. Next morning, however, he found himself alone and to his horror, in a stinking cell in a local police station. Unable to speak Greek, George was horrified to find himself in such a situation although he was not entirely unfamiliar with those surroundings. Over the years, as a hobo and a drunk, in various cities around the world, he had been in a prison cell many times. In fact he felt relieved to find himself in the cell. It meant a night's sleep, out of harm's way and out of the howling wind and rain and all other sorts of unpleasantness that might otherwise had befallen him. However, to his horror, he had been charged with indecent assault. A local youth, a member of a gang of boys, told his parents that old George said he would like to commit a sexual act. George denied the allegation and claimed that his park-bench acquaintance must have been the person responsible. Old George said his drinking companion that afternoon was as far as he could remember, either German or Dutch, and that he said he was an ex-merchant seaman. Although it was common to share a bottle, you never knew who the other person was.

Old George told the court, through the translator, that the other man, whom he knew only for a few hours, was an odd character who had commented in broken English about his sexual feelings towards the very young, pointing to the young girls playing hide and seek nearby, that if they was old enough to bleed they was old enough to have sex. This remark convinced George that it had indeed been the disturbed individual who had caused him to end up in a Greek jail, sentenced to seven years imprisonment. In the wrong place at the wrong time, he said, but was unable to prove his innocence. In prison he turned the situation to his advantage, by learning Greek, pigeon fashion allowing him to converse with his fellow inmates.

Books became his friend; even today he said, books are best, a man can rely on them. His incarceration led him to get off the drink. Arriving in England around 1950 he had missed the war years, although he said that, at one time, he would probably have joined the French Foreign Legion. His physical fitness and size meant they would have welcomed him with open arms.

For the last fifteen years or so he never settled down with anyone special. He was a natural ladies' man in the making. On more than one occasion I saw him with different middle age women, walking arm in arm, they were engrossed in his every word. In winter he would often take off to Paris where he stayed for free, working at the well-known second-hand bookshop called 'Shakespeare's'. The owner, also an American, provided accommodation for drifters in an upstairs room furnished with mattresses on the floor. He told me you could stay there free for a month or two and that if ever I or my friends found myself in Paris I should seek out this venue, using 'old George' as a point of reference.

In stark contrast to old George was John Tabernacle. At just over six foot he towered over the rest of us. His distinguished angular features, jet black shoulder length hair and the airs and graces that matched his ex-public school persona, evoked a bygone age. Out of all of us John didn't wear the outfit of a deckchair attendant comfortably. He had a pronounced stoop that made the jacket appear ill-fitting, which led a few members of the public to ridicule him. However, if anyone mocked him they felt the wrath of our anger.

John Tabernacle was affectionately known as Long John, I suppose after Long John Baldry, the former member of Manfred Mann, in the early sixties. Long John had a reputation for his vast knowledge of hymns and classical music. He once gave us a rendition of his musical skills by performing on an old iron-framed piano, in a pub in George Street, in the heart of the Hastings Old Town. I missed the performance as I was otherwise occupied with a girl from Denmark or Sweden, probably wedged between two fishing boats, trying to have my wicked way. The public were mesmerized by his piano playing.

Long John decided to spend this particular summer holiday as a deckchair attendant, lodging with friends at nearby Winchelsea Beach, cycling backwards and forwards and still arriving at work on time. A deeply religious man and a former University Don, or so we were told. Around thirty years of age, he was seeking solace but also wanted to be part of humanity on his own terms. While the general consensus was that he appeared strange, the general public reckoned he was a likeable and well-mannered fellow, as opposed to a real low-down bum. At the end of the season he rented an apartment near the World's End, off the Kings road in London, where he wrote contemporary religious musical recitals, which he performed publicly.

Harvey's pitch consisted of 150-200 deckchairs; it was the smallest of the pitches allocated. His rimmed spectacles were usually balanced on the end of his nose. He had a mop of snow-white hair, Nordic features and a pronounced pointed chin. Of Welsh descent, Cardiff to be precise, he wore the casual attire: khaki jacket, jeans, sandals, a white shirt and a run-of-the-mill striped tie. On his right arm, above the elbow, he wore a plain two-inch wide black mourning-band. He could see I was curious about the arm-band so he explained why he wore it all the time. He was a gentle soul of 70 or so, by far the oldest of all employees that summer. Hastings Borough Council held the old man in high esteem, as did all the holidaymakers who came into contact with him. The armband was in memory of his late wife, a senior nurse who had just been appointed matron at a local hospital; she died 32 years earlier, as a result of an aneurysm, on his return from his part time job he found her lifeless laying on the kitchen floor.

Harvey was a deeply religious man who kept his own counsel, mostly but on this occasion he released his innermost feelings of sorrow for us all to witness. With tears in his eyes he explained that, after this tragedy, his life became a torment and his thoughts turned to suicide. He swore himself to a life of chastity, so determined was he to remain faithful to the memory of his deceased wife, in mind and body. How could he wear the armband of mourning, yet find himself in the arms of another? It would have been hypocrisy he cried out in his broad Welsh accent. Now with a gambling habit confined to horse racing, throughout the working day he would be seen heading towards the Memorial, past the clock tower and into the nearest bookmakers. The council, his employer, turned a blind eye to these disappearances. They had no wish to upset Harvey; by now he was a household name, as for the last twenty years or so Hastings had become his second home, deck-chair employment in the summer and casual work in the winter working for a furniture removal company. In Wales it was rumored that he had inherited an old farmhouse but this had been sold to pay for his gambling debts. All monies left over had been given to the Catholic Church.

Immersed in thought he dabbed his eyes with a white, newly-pressed cotton handkerchief. He had drunk a few too many he claimed, and that his defences were down, at which he removed himself from the table and retreated towards the toilets. We all looked at each other. Not one of us made a derogatory or pitying remark. Courtesy was the thing to offer him. He returned soon after, having washed his face. Waving his hands in the air he claimed that drying hands on towels in public toilets wasn't the right and proper thing to do; natural air drying was the most hygienic method.

Our table became a little raucous, not in a bad or argumentative way but with a fair amount of bad language being bandied around the table. Long John and Harvey, being religious, had most in common and agreed to keep in touch through a Post Office Box (post restante) but whether or not they would stick to their agreement was anyone's guess.

The dynamics of this particular Sunday evening were chaotic to say the least.

Richard and Mark were also members of our group. They were polar opposites, Richard, long black hair, showed a keen interest in music and played the guitar. Mark was more reserved, more monosyllabic or just a grunt, both were in their mid-forty's. They were devoted to each other as seen when given the opportunity they would for a brief moment hold hands and become tactile but only in our company, homosexuality only having been recently legalised. If gossip were to be believed they met in prison; one had served sentences for mail-order fraud, the other a prison warden. Which form of gossip was true no one knew, but certainly they hadn't been involved in anything nefarious or questionable, with regard to their daily cash takings as deckchair attendants, unlike one character, who started work on a Monday, selling adult tickets but issued O.A.P and children's on receipt so pocketing the difference. His fraud was found out by an inspector, doing spot checks on a Saturday, the busiest day of the week, the thief, aware of being caught, left the ticket machine and the standard work issue, khaki jacket, with an innocent elderly couple of holiday makers, unaware of his ruse, then fled pocketing the day's takings. Richard was also rumoured to have been a happily married man without children, a very witty funny man and gregarious, while Mark the more studious and serious. Their paths had crossed and led to a relationship which, at that particular time, had to remain behind closed doors for fear of the legal and physical consequences.

Their future plans involved buying a second-hand, ex-Government Ambulance, converted into a motor home and going overland to India then onto Australia and finally America. How they were funding the trip they never divulged, and neither did we enquire. The one factor I observed was that, unlike many others, our group never seemed to disparage another character or bad-mouth them. The mantra of the Drifters was 'live and let live', for there but by the grace of God go I. We all agreed on this sentiment, as Bob Dylan rightly observed: 'The times they are a changing.'

The mid nineteen-sixties were proving just that. No politician of any persuasion could halt the tide of nature, ebbing and flowing into different styles. We lost our deference toward our predecessors. It was the last generation of the followers, to the leaders. The underclass could now be of any class; the class structures of Great Britain appeared to be breaking up.

When 'last-orders' were called, any money left in the kitty was shared out. It was time for us to go our separate ways, with handshakes all around and hopes to 'See you on the road sometime'. Our parting of the ways was as normal as if it had been any other Sunday evening. This, of course, was probably the last time I would be fortunate enough to have been in the company of such fine individuals.

FOLLOW MY INSTINCT

I was alone, walking through the maze of alleyways and steps that led towards the West Hill of Hastings, my heart had sunk to an all-time low. I was now without my friends, work and still an unhappy home life. What was to become of me? I asked myself, as I hurried homeward.

Suddenly I became aware of someone calling me, Nicky and Annabella, two teenage girls I had known for a few years. They were around the same age as me, afraid of the dark and they wanted me to walk them home.

My spirits lifted at the sight of the girls, although I'd never been in a physical relationship with either girl, although there had been a fair amount of banter and frivolous flirting between us, but nothing serious. Annabella, the taller of the two and of Italian descent, asked what I was going to do now that winter was on its way.

'You've lost out on having fun with the girls at the 'Pam-Dor' coffee bar. Now that those foreign girls have gone home, there's no chance of any of us keeping you warm, you traitor Zac, that's what you are, I'm only joking.' she laughed.

'Yes,' I replied, 'you have a point. I need to think about my present situation.' I scratched my head.

Suddenly it came to me. 'I've got it! I know what I'll do; I'll take off for Sweden, that's what I'll do. I've got an address of someone; she is bound to let me stay with her, maybe get a job working at her parent's farm. Thanks Annabella. I now know where my future lies. I'm going to hit the road and travel like the low-down bums, become one of them. I've made up my mind so no going back, I am determined.'

They looked at me aghast. 'You must be joking, you are not even eighteen.'

Taunting me the girls said that I was all talk and that in a year or two I would be married to a local girl, with a secure job and children in tow. I replied that they were safe; they weren't my type and that it was blondes who had all the fun, just look at Marilyn Monroe. That put a stop to their cackling but they ended up insisting we carry on walking, our arms linked, me in the middle, a rose between two thorns I announced. We were in fits of laughter as we arrived at 'Wallinger's Walk', close to the graveyard, where Nicky lived with her mother. Annabella and I continued on to her home, off Priory road where her parents lived, with its formidable view facing the East Hill, in the direction of Folkestone and Dover, the gateway to Europe.

About three weeks passed with little inclination to find work. I knew if I did I would be trapped. I had received my week-in-hand from the council, which helped pay for my keep at home. By this time I had built up a decent sum in my Post Office savings account, having worked a seven-day week for Hastings Borough Council for months.

THE PACKAGE ARRIVES

My father said little, most of the time; it was my mother who had the loudest voice in the house. Over breakfast one day she said, aggressively: 'Well, you've got what you want. It's arrived. The postman's just been and I have signed the registered packet on your behalf. So when you can be bothered to come downstairs you can show it to me.'

It was only eight fifteen, I replied 'I'll be down in a minute'.

Yes, there it was, on the kitchen table, tearing open the well-sealed package, under my mother's watchful eye, I gave a sigh of relief. It was all mine, that black leather gold-tooled book, my five year passport to freedom. Here I come, I rejoiced to myself. It was unusual to be granted such a legal document while still not 18 years of age. It was down to my new social worker who had intervened on my behalf. I had told the social worker I was thinking of going to Israel to work on a Kibbutz; which she referred to her notes saying, 'It's obvious you want to go to Israel as you are a fully-fledged Jew from your mother's womb' For the first time I was curious about my birth mother.'

She reiterated, 'Unlike the freedom you have Zac, your mother was, as far as we understand, a sixteen-year old Jewish refugee in a Nazi German concentration camp, befriended by a young German soldier who found her physical adolescent maturity rewarding, in agreement with a colleague who admitted that he also was under her spell, finding her physical attractiveness conducive to his taste. The latter working in the administration department relating to date of births and ethnicity, he altered her date of birth, where records showed her two years younger than she was, to escape the Gas Chamber, as the eldest go first'.

For the first time in my life, I am not under the control of the Social Workers department, with whom I was grateful for their integrity shown towards me and the first time I had found out anything about my birth mother.

The cut-out rectangular window on the passport cover, highlighted my name of Zechariah Cohen, not my mother's former married English name, as just after the Second World War she married after a whirlwind romance but things ended badly between them, he was caught and imprisoned for stealing fuel, while in the armed forces, so it was said. The truth is I don't know what happened between them. I do know that while she was pregnant and waiting to give birth to me, she walked the streets of London, homeless with her other child, my elder brother Luke, who was two years my senior. She was detained by the authorities, Luke was put into care somewhere, as was I also soon after my birth. In the meantime she had met an Irishman and had gone to live in Glasgow, in the well-known Gorbals area, with the young man's family parents and grandparents.

My mother's outspoken views, her chaotic lifestyle, and her flirtatious and lustful ways towards men caused havoc among the local Irish Catholic community. As a result she was ostracized by her neighbours, and physically and emotionally abused by her partner. I ended up in a Barnardos home for orphans in Surrey, one of the 'Sunshine children', whose pictures would be a government initiative advertised in national newspapers. Up for adoption, here or in Australia, where, for the cost of ten pounds a government initiative planned to send mostly orphan boys as a cheap form of labour, working on farms. I was sent to at least three temporary placements on a trial owing to a severe speech impediment, a nervous disposition, with an enquiring mind, asking questions all the time.

'Nice boy but not for us', so sent back to the orphanage until at around four years old, I was taken into the family of Mr. and Mrs. Marshall, whereas in all probabilities, if they had not taken me in, I would have remained at the children's home for the long term. Few adoptees favoured the older child, too set in their ways, they said, preferring a new born baby.

And so it was that in October 1967, in the so-called prime of my life, fit, healthy and full of the spirit of adventure, I was ready to take on any challenges life had to throw at me, including that of learning Swedish, fending for myself and adjusting to the Nordic lifestyle. I kept in contact by letter, with a girl by the name of Karen from a previous summer holiday romance, with whom I had not got past the heavy petting stage. Letters sent between us arranged that I would work on her parent's farm, a few miles from Gavle, a town 200 kilometers north of Stockholm. Gripping my passport tightly in my hand, with high expectations in my heart and £50.00 in travellers' cheques in my wallet, the amount needed to enter Sweden; I was ready to embark on my great adventure...

END OF BOOK ONE